I am Eagle!

BLACK STAR, LONDON

I am Eagle!

GHERMAN TITOV [Stepanovich]
and
MARTIN CAIDIN

Based on interviews with

Wilfred Burchett and

Red → Anthony Purdy

THE **BOBBS-MERRILL** COMPANY, INC.
A SUBSIDIARY OF HOWARD W. SAMS & CO., INC.
Publishers · INDIANAPOLIS · NEW YORK

Contents

Introduction

During the evening of August 5th, 1961, radio engineers, announcers, officials and other personnel of Radio Moscow began to converge in the studios of the official Soviet radio station in Moscow. During the night the number of people in the studios grew; many members of the regular daytime staff completed their work for the day, but did not leave the building. Through the night the people gathered in small groups, listening intently as the head officials of Radio Moscow gathered in Studio One, and received a series of special telephone calls.

Through the night the calls came in, one after the other. They were from an elaborate electronic and communications center, hundreds of miles from Moscow. Each telephone report brought hopeful smiles from the nervous audience in the studios high over the Russian capitol. The news was of a countdown, an elaborate and exhaustive electronic orchestration that had been under way for several days at an isolated area called Baikonur.

The successive calls reflected the confidence of the thousands of people at Baikonur, confidence that grew with the elimination of hundreds of major electronic and mechanical obstacles with an immense rocket. The calls reported of many things; of direct contact through an international shortwave radio system with small ships strung across the Atlantic and Pacific Oceans . . . of the slow and ponderous movement of a giant steel tower from its position

7

of embracing the rocket . . . of weather reports from around the entire planet . . . of many technical items all of which blended together steadily into a confusing but, to the informed, a superbly coordinated kaleidoscope.

Most of the activities concerned with this evening took place in the heart of the Soviet Union. The outside world was not invited to participate in the events, nor were they able even to witness the proceedings, a situation unlike that surrounding Lt. Col. John Glenn's flight in February, 1962. Baikonur was not unfamiliar to many people beyond the borders of Russia, but its characteristics, its role as the Soviet gateway to the vast reaches beyond our planet, remained essentially the knowledge of an elite group of Russians, and no one else.

On this evening, as the hours passed, the Soviet Union prepared to make an enormous step outward from the earth. In essence, it was the first true Seven-League Boots' stride away from the world. The Russians did not invite a scrutiny of their activities before the fact and, indeed, did their best to assure a privacy from the rest of an inquisitive, awed, and somewhat frightened world.

Yet complete secrecy was impossible to attain. Although the people of the world knew nothing of the steps being taken to send one of their own away from his planet of birth, many men were entirely aware of what transpired at Baikonur. It is a fact of this new age of space that electronic secrecy is a goal to be cherished but rarely attained. Russian ships in the Atlantic and the Pacific tested their communications with home stations. Along a variety of radio bands they sent and received messages with the Soviet Union. They checked and rechecked their ability to receive electronically-coded bits of information from an object that soon—they hoped—would hurtle in absolute silence through the sea of space far over their vessels.

Each vessel ascertained that it cruised in a position that agreed exactly with a preassigned latitude and longitude across the earth's liquid surface. Navigators aboard the ships studied the stars, while their communications counterparts nodded to anxious scientists that, radio-wise,, everything stood in readiness for the event.

No Russian spoke a word publicly of these ships. But American aircraft and American warships plotted, tracked, and pursued with their own devices these Soviet vessels. They knew the size, weight, speed, capacity, equipment and purpose of their cold-war opponents that hove to in the open seas. They had followed on radar screens the movement of the vessels from the first moments that they departed their home ports. They followed them with cameras and radar as they steamed into North African ports to take on supplies, and then sailed on to their assigned locations on the seas.

So there was no secret—except to the great massed public of the world, which knew little or nothing about the stupendous event that was soon to happen. It is interesting to speculate on the whys of this ignorance of the impending event; certainly the fact of the Russian vessels at sea was not a secret; their presence and their mission was known clearly. Officially, however, nothing was said.

The hours passed, and at Baikonur the first light of dawn streaked the horizon. Still the electronic destruction of minutes and seconds continued. Planned events and sequences of events moved smoothly. Minor problems cropped up, but efficient and experienced engineers eliminated these swiftly. A countdown was in progress. It was a good one; in the lexicon of this new age, one could accurately say "it was a damned good count . . ."

A man, garbed in an outlandish costume and an even more grotesque helmet, stepped down from a small bus at Baikonur. The suit enclosing his body sealed him in tightly; to breathe and to escape stewing in his own perspiration he carried a small container. Batteries discharged their current in this object to feed cooling air into and throughout the suit to assure the comfort of its wearer. The man shuffled slightly as he walked, encumbered by his attire that was designed for a world where men could not live.

A half-dozen steps behind him, similarly garbed, externally identical, another man shuffled along. The second in line was a standby, an alternate; on the slim possibility that the first man might trip as he stepped off the bus, might twist an ankle, might suffer even the slightest injury, the second man would simply move ahead and replace the other.

But there was no slip, no injury, not the slightest of problems. Accompanied by his alter ego, shuffling to a chorus of cheers and applause, the man disappeared within the ribs of a waiting elevator. Motors whined, cables stretched taut, and the men ascended many stories above the ground. They looked for miles across the Russian landscape, then walked along a steel platform. Waiting technicians worked rapidly through final checkouts and studies; in the minutes following they assisted the first man in entering a massive metal cubicle. His standby nodded in satisfaction, and asked to have his helmet removed.

The stage was set. In the intervening minutes, less than a hundred minutes away, the drama would draw to a fiery climax that was, paradoxically, only the opening instant of an even greater wonder that would begin on a pillar of blinding flame.

The climax came, the new chapter opened, and men screamed and shouted in jubilation. The source of their open-mouthed and wide-eyed wonder blazed a streak in the heavens and clawed its way against the massive gravity of the earth into the vacuum beyond our air oceans. Then flame blinked out, and a miracle was begun.

The first *journey* of the Age of Space was launched.

Several hours later—hours in which every minute would be inscribed in the pages of man's adventures—a man named Yuri Levatin shifted in his chair until he was comfortable. He sat before a desk on which there stood two squat black microphones, a desk in Studio One of Radio Moscow, in the heart of the Soviet capitol. As quickly as he would soon speak, other men, as well as women, would repeat his words in forty-four different languages. Their broadcasts, all to follow immediately behind that of Levatin, would sweep most of the planet's lands where men lived and could listen to radios.

Levatin glanced at the wall clock and cleared his throat. He glanced at a glass dial beneath the clock, and started imperceptibly when a light flashed red. Then, slowly and deliberately, he began:

"This is Radio Moscow. A Tass statement announces that at nine A.M. *Moscow time today a satellite spaceship, Vostok II, was launched into orbit around the earth. The ship is piloted by Pilot-Cosmonaut Gherman Stephanovitch Titov . . ."*

Levatin continued his broadcast; he spoke of Titov again and again, opening a barrage of millions of words about this young Russian whose name overnight would be on the lips of every thinking human being in the world. As the hours passed, the full impact of what was happening in the blackness of space far above the earth began to sink into the minds of men everywhere.

This was not a space shot. It was not a quick test flight, a brief culmination of a long preparation that was almost anti-climactic in its rapid conclusion. Gherman Titov was not only in space; he was *remaining* in space. Titov was not bound on a single circuit of the world; he was defying fatalistic predictions and continuing a fantastic journey—one destined to be remembered forever, and everywhere.

In the ensuing hours, Moscow, Stalingrad, Baikonur, Leningrad —all Russia's cities, towns, villages, went wild with joy. In the bigger cities, where crowds massed on the streets to hear repeated again and again the triumphant bulletins, the normal pace of life snarled to a crawl. Spontaneously, people flew banners from win-

dows, danced in the streets, stopped foreigners on the sidewalks
to ask in breathless queries if the vistors had heard of the miracle
that was going on over their heads.

Foreign newsmen, from nations around the world, watched the
celebrations and the shouted cries of shared triumph. They went
back to their offices and wrote long sheets of copy. At this moment,
for many moments to come, no matter what else might be going
on within their country or around the world, the individual Russian and all his fellows enjoy with a rich satisfaction another victory of their country in the new world of space. Many of them
understand little, or perhaps nothing, of the import of the flight.
They understand little about the mechanics of what is happening,
and they can not care less.

He was moving with tremendous speed, was Titov—at eighteen
thousand miles per hour. That was enough to know. He was in
space—and that was a miracle by itself. He was *remaining* in space,
and who asks for detailed analyses of such a miracle? He was in a
spaceship that had been predicted—as every Russian who could
and did read knew well—by the Father of flight in space, Kon-
stantin E. Tsiolkovskii himself. With all these things to know and
about which one could marvel, understanding took a back seat to
awe and wonder and fierce jubilation.

The morning of August 6th ticked by. The minutes dragged and
the hours became interminable. And still Titov whirled around
the planet, plunging through space in a dizzying fall around the
world that continued for hour after hour, falling forever, plunging
in vacuum with a speed of three hundred miles every minute—
five miles every second!

The people on the surface of the earth, flattened to the surface
of their world by gravity, did not wonder in ignorance as to the
safety of their new hero. For Titov was anything but silent. Completely weightless, dropping through space without any support,
watching in awe the miracles of days and nights that were only
forty-five minutes each in length, the new Russian spaceman be-

came swept up with the incredible wonder of it all. He talked and called to earth. His face appeared on television screens, flashed down from vacuum, knifing through the multiple layers of the atmosphere, a visual presentation of the miracle.

And completely carried away by it all, his voice crying out in sheer joy, Titov shouted to all mankind, *"I am Eagle! I am Eagle! . . ."*

Radio Moscow poured out the reports. A well coordinated propaganda machine selected its prepackaged groups of biographical material, and smoothly the men and women of the Soviet information machine carved the image of Titov. The task presented little more difficulty than might be encountered in any communications problems of broadcasting—for the public, in Russia and elsewhere, thirsted avidly for news. Moscow slaked the thirst with a barrage of material that spoke clearly for its own, long preparations.

The tone of the broadcasts from Levatin, and the other announcers, clearly revealed the growing confidence in Titov's performance, his safety, his ultimate successful return to the surface of the world. *"Cosmonaut Titov feels fine . . . two-way radio communications are working well . . . flying over Africa Major Titov sends greetings to the people of Africa from Vostok II . . . the flight plan is being carried out as scheduled . . ."*

And indeed it was. Twenty-five hours and eighteen minutes following his departure, Gherman Titov returned to earth. The first journey through space of more than 435,000 miles was now a fact. One could almost say that the deafening cheers and roars of the Russians carried as an echo several times around the globe, with all the speed that Titov had achieved himself in the vacuum beyond our planet.

This book is the story of Gherman Stephanovitch Titov, of his journey in the spaceship called Vostok II, of his life, his family, and of the many things that relate to this telling. In this introduction, it is my responsibility to establish clearly the manner of its telling to the reader.

As the credits of authorship clearly define, the story was re-searched within the Soviet Union by Wilfred Burchett and An-thony Purdy. There is no question—not any at all—that their story of Titov is authentic.

Before this manuscript reached its first page, I had several top engineers in our own missile and space fields study the notes ob-tained by us from Burchett and Purdy. In them lay a book of tremendous import to Americans.

Each person felt that this story *must be told*. They said to me that speed was essential in its telling.

I have in this book separated the wheat from the chaff. I have done so beneath the watchful eye of engineers who at my request and by their own nature are extraordinarily critical.

The two researchers—Burchett and Purdy—in the past had con-ducted a major series of interviews with the first man ever to reach into space: Yuri Alekseyevich Gagarin. Later, after Titov's spec-tacular voyage about our planet, they met with the second cosmo-naut in the big conference room of the State Committee for Cultural Relations in Moscow. There, in the high-ceilinged room with its elaborate chandeliers, they discussed with the Russian spaceman his training, his flight, his reactions. The material they have gathered in these talks is unprecedented; much of it is com-pletely exclusive. And beyond question Burchett and Purdy have managed to set down on paper more of the side issues of space flight—the human issues—than has ever been provided before on the Russians.

They described their first impression of Titov with the remark that he was greatly similar to his predecessor, Gagarin. "Short, compact, tough; both obviously good-humored . . ." Perceptive American correspondents corroborate such an impression. One American newsman, who has reported on the space age from before its inception, was careful to describe to me both Gagarin and Titov as "men of obvious great intelligence and capabilities . . ." He places them precisely on the same plane and level as our own astronauts; knowing both the Russians and the Americans, he hastens to add that there is less of a sense of frustration with the cosmonauts than is suffered by their American contemporaries. Which is understandable.

When asked about his feelings toward his flight—what he thought about his own safety because of traveling at 18,000 miles per hour—Titov asserted that his faith was in the men and the machines who produced his Vostok, in the doctors and the scientists who monitored and controlled his flight. He stated that he was as certain that he would complete his flight safely as if he had been traveling on a bus in Moscow.

Such statements have been attacked in the American press as Titov being representative of the Russians who sneer at God, who place their faith in machines rather than in the heavens. The remarks reflect poorly upon our critics, for our own astronauts have made statements similar to those of Titov, and the similarity is quite astounding. But there erupts little criticism when voiced in this country, while such words coming from a Russian spaceman are catalysts to violent outcries. It is difficult at times to wonder about our perception and objectivity under these circumstances, for it is obvious that we are smarting under our own problems, and loath to admit publicly a clear and definite man-in-space lead and superiority as is currently enjoyed by the Russians.

Titov's answers to his Communist interviewers were marked by a sharp matter-of-factness that has aided us considerably in this story. He spoke directly and, throughout the long discussions with the cosmonaut, Titov was careful not to be evasive to questions that otherwise might be regarded as designed to put him off balance. At times his overwhelming enthusiasm for his space mission resulted in waving his arms about with animation to describe various scenes and events.

To assist in the clear presentation of many details, Titov's aide —a captain assigned to the task of assisting Titov—brought to the conference room hundreds of questions that had been asked by previous newsmen, and also their answers. Titov himself did not refer to these papers, but provided them for whatever assistance they might be to Burchett and Purdy.

Titov's conversation extended from his boyhood in Siberia to his wife's reluctance at his mission; he spoke with an awe of the genius of the man who built his spaceship—the Chief Constructor. He described his acute disappointment when Gagarin—and not himself—received the word that he would be the first man into space. And his mood became intent and thoughtful when he spoke of the twenty-five hours in which he watched the sun sweep its colors of dawn seventeen times across the face of the globe.

A clearer picture of Titov emerged steadily during the interviews. Small items revealed more of the man than the cosmonaut. As a youngster he hoped to become a flier—and later he became a crack jet pilot. Against family objections he finally entered military service—and ended up in space. There were obstacles other than family reluctance—his wife's objections, a broken arm that resulted in a long and painful healing process, and, during his training, black marks for his short temper and an incident in which he was severely criticized for his "irresponsibility."

And perhaps most indicative of his sharp candor was his description of the moment in space when, passing over Japan, he heard a broadcast in the Russian language that was being directed to him. "It was in very bad Russian," he laughed, "but I could make out, quite clearly, that it was directed to me. They—on the ground— were talking about God and of angels and of the heavens. I looked through the window of the spaceship and thought that if there was a God here, I couldn't see Him. I regretted that I could not talk back to those people on the ground; despite their attitudes about God and angels and heaven they were, after all, praying *for* me."

This is the story of the first man ever to make a voyage through space: Major Gherman Stephanovitch Titov . . .

MARTIN CAIDIN

Cape Canaveral, 1962

I am Eagle!

1. Prologue

Near the southeastern border of the Soviet Union, bordering Mongolia and China, lies the small village of Polkovnikovo. Like the other villages and towns in this forested area, more than two thousand miles from the Russian capitol, Polkovnikovo is a gathering of cabins built of rounded logs. Because of the fierce Siberian winters that slash cruelly against the small communities, the cabins are all linked together by wooden fences. It is a town in which life is shared closely; a necessity of farming, of mutual assistance in the terrible winter storms, a natural result of the close community life that prevails.

The name Siberia is synonymous with bitter cold and an impression of eternal snow and ice; a land hostile to its inhabitants, a land that is regarded almost universally as fit only for exiles. It is cold in Siberia and the winters are bitter; it is not true, however, that these conditions prevail the year around or that the people who live here—as did their forefathers for many decades—are at all anxious to leave. Siberia, especially the countryside of Polkovnikovo, is a paradox of conditions.

The land is, above all else, surprising in its beauty and in its riches. Vast tracts of woodland spread for hundreds of miles, an array of blankets of silver birch and snow-sprayed firs that stand strongly against the worst of the cold and the winds. It is rich in its streams, and its rolling hills have been tamed by generations of farmers to whom hardship is simply a way of life that has been lived for so long that they are in contempt of those people who have never known the joy of living so closely with soil and nature.

The summers are warm, and the air almost sings with the creatures of nature that abound in the seasonal warmth and the brilliant sun. During these months of farm weather, the people work the week through. They take advantage of the lull in the violence of weather to which they are so accustomed. So long as the sun is warm and the countryside green, the people work. All day long they toil in the fields, growing, reaping, harvesting; they know full well that when winter comes, these things will be impossible. Because the life here can quickly become a fight for survival, they work closely with one another, sharing their goods and their blessings, denying no one who is deserving of any assistance they may ask in a time of need.

Even during the long winter months the country is beautiful. The snow is deep, but the forests are alive with the firs and the gleaming light of the sun flashing down on the white earth.

It is not always like this, of course. The Siberian winters are infamous, and with good reason. The great northern winds at times rage down from the mountains with little warning. Even those people who have lived through many winters are caught unawares by the speed with which the storms thunder down upon the villages and homes.

The winds gather their strength along the steppes in the Arctic. They sweep cold and snow together in an atmospheric avalanche that shrieks across the countryside like a tidal wave of freezing air and snow, swirling together as a single mass. When it strikes, the sound is as if a locomotive were roaring only feet away from the ears of a man; a pounding wave of thunder and wind. Immediately it strikes visibility from the air. Sunlight and trees and mountains are blotted out by a blinding white blanket so intense that a man often cannot see his hand before his face.

A storm like this struck the village of Polkovnikovo in the

'forties. Six boys and girls were walking along a road that wound through the forests when, without warning, the storm howled down upon them. Instantly the children were blinded by the storm. They could not see the road on which they stood, or even the high trees bordering the road. They stood in a tight circle, helpless, their heads turned inward, their arms linked together for safety. This was common sense; this was survival, to stand thus and wait for the onslaught to abate, for vision to return to them.

But the storm whipped the winds faster and faster. Long minutes later the children were beginning to freeze. Their faces were becoming dangerously cold, their limbs gained an alarming stiffness.

To continue standing was to court death by freezing. But what could they do? It was impossible to see anywhere. One of the two boys in the group took charge. He insisted they must reach shelter or they were certain to die. The others protested; it was madness to try and walk to any destination in a storm that blinded them.

The boy shouted angrily at them. He turned around slowly until the icy wind slashed directly at his face from the front. The wind was from the north; knowing this, he could work out the direction of the village. He told the others to link their hands tightly, to move together in a file. Heads down, the small group struggled into the wind. Every few minutes they stopped, to rub each others faces briskly with their mittens.

Their cheeks had become white and "dead." The skin was frozen. The children scooped up snow, rubbing the snow against their faces. They trudged on and on, the boy in the lead judging his direction by the constant wind. Long minutes later, numb and almost frozen, he stumbled against a fence. He shouted the news to the others. At once they all moved against the fence, guiding themselves to the house they knew must be near. An incredulous farmer and his wife opened the door as they reached the house and pounded for entrance.

The six children had been given up as lost. Storms such as this had claimed the lives of grown, experienced woodsmen. For six children to survive, to walk out of such a storm, was unheard of. The story of their survival spread through the village, and then through the countryside. People everywhere talked of the young lad who had saved himself and the others.

His name was Gherman—Gherman Stephanovitch Titov.

The Altai region of Siberia covers an area roughly the size of England. In the latter half of the nineteenth century the vast tracts of woodlands, and the mountains where the national treasury was fed by the Imperial mines of gold and silver, were the personal preserves of the Tsars. Altai to them was a headache. They needed the precious ore that they mined with political prisoners, and they needed an agricultural society with which their labor forces could be fed and supported.

The Tsars moved carefully. They created a legend about Altai —a legend of rich and abundant farmlands, of land ready for the asking by any families who wished to settle in the region. Hundreds of thousands of peasants and their families, suffering from economic hardship and political oppression in European Russia, followed the lure of the new land to the east. Entire villages as a single group abandoned their homes, packed their goods on sleds and carts, and began the long trek to the east. Those who could not afford to own horses, carried their belongings on their backs. Men, women and children trudged over the hundreds of miles, traveling eastward, spurred on by the golden promises of the Tsars. The road they traveled was the one over which—years later— would be built the Trans-Siberian railway. But in those days only the rough road could be used as the path to their "promised land."

One of the men who fought his way to a land where he could till his own soil, own his own land, was Ivan Leontovich Titov— the great grandfather of the boy who would one day by his wits and his courage save the lives of six children in a howling Siberian snowstorm. His story is important to us. It is from the fiber of men such as these, and the cruel hardships they endured over four generations, that was produced the young man who was one day to become known to all mankind as the first man ever to make a sustained flight in the vacuum beyond this planet.

The family story of the Titovs does not look back upon Gherman's great grandfather as one to remember fondly. Thousands of the people with whom Ivan Titov traveled never reached their land of golden promise. They fell like flies from hunger, exhaustion, disease and the savage cold along the way. Other thousands despaired as their children, who suffered the worst of all, either fell ill, or died; these folk simply abandoned the long journey and settled wherever they might find enough food to remain alive.

Yet, thousands did fight their way to the Altai region. Here the bitter deception of the Tsars struck in terrible fury at them. There was no land available; it had already been parceled out by the Tsars to their political favorites.

Ivan Titov raged in his helpless anger. His dreams of his own land vanished against the reality of slaving at the mines, or working with no more rights than an animal for the few landowners. Embittered, stripped of his faith in his fellow men, he cursed and denounced God. A deeply religious man all his life, he now spurned God and spat on the church.

He died a dozen years later when his son was barely eleven years old, leaving with the boy a memory of stark hatred, of bitterness. His legacy to his son was scarcely better than he had known.

The Siberian legends that persist today grew from these times, and they need little exaggeration to fit the tales of hardship that remained through the years. The winter cold plunged often to sixty degrees below zero. For weeks on end the temperature remained far below zero, and for almost half the year the country lay buried in deep white drifts. The northern blizzards slashed at the crude cabins, blotting out all traces of roads or buildings, shrouding in white anonymity the hapless souls trapped in the open. In the winter no man's life was safe if he traveled over the countryside. Through the forests ran packs of wolves. Made ravenous by the winters that destroyed the other animals, or forced them to seclusion, the starved wolves turned with a savage hunger against man. During the worst winters no man was safe even within the villages, for the big, gaunt animals ghosted among the log cabins, their hunger overcoming their natural fear of man's habitat.

And always present to drain the spirit of any man was his servitude to the landowners. There existed no hope of improving a family's life except through special grants. The peasants were literally slaves, and they lived as such. They could be destroyed at the whim of the landowners, and not infrequently a man who incurred the wrath of these lordly figures suffered death—either directly or by banishment.

Ivan Titov's son knew little better than his father, until the year 1917. War swept across Europe; with war came the igniting of long-suppressed emotions, the freeing of political hopes, the lashing of subdued emotions. In 1917, the Bolsheviks seized power. A wave of violence flamed through the Altai regions, and here the peasants flung themselves uncontrollably at their masters.

The landowners died quickly. Entire families were cut to pieces; in their rage the peasants hacked their bodies with knives, smashed their bones with clubs, mangled and garrotted and killed in the inevitable bloodletting. Then, in response to the ever-present hunger of their existence, they turned back to the land. Not for their Tsarist masters any longer, but for themselves.

They divided the land among the villagers. A decade before Josef Stalin began his drive to create the vast collective farms that now spread across the Russian countryside, the Altai peasants formed their own communes, patterned around the ancient Biblical societies. The first of these new communes near the village of Polkovnikovo was called *May Morning*. It was the home of a ten-year old boy named Stefan Titov.

He formed the link from the past to the future. Grandson of the embittered peasant Ivan Titov, Stefan was to become the father of the future spaceman—his son, Gherman. My two researchers, Burchett and Purdy, lived for several days with the Titov family. Gherman's father remembers clearly those early days when the land finally did become theirs . . .

"The first thing we had to do," he recalls, "was to create a community with some substance. We worked together, the parents and every child who could help. We built large, two-storied log cabins in which three to four families could live. The average family thus gained two rooms and a separate kitchen, but little cooking was ever done at home. In those short summer months when there was so much to be done, we worked seven days a week, from sunup to sundown. We ate our meals in the fields, right where we worked. I can still remember what a giant of a man we had for a cook. I thought his voice could be heard all over Siberia. And in the winter, we gathered together in a large dining hall, so the cooks could pool their labor.

"Everyone contributed what he had to the commune. My father Pavel owned a horse, but had no land. Mikhail Nosov had some land but no horse. Some had farm tools; others didn't. Everything was brought together to the commune and, after that, all we needed were the people to work. We had that, all right! We had all been working like slaves for so long that it was a pleasure to go out and do a full day's honest work—and it didn't matter how hard it was. We were, after all, finally working for ourselves. We felt as if Ivan Titov's dream had finally come true.

"Immediately the commune built a small school for the first three classes. Almost all the children and most of the adults were illiterates. You could see three generations—grandfather, father, and son—all sitting together and struggling to learn the fundamentals of spelling and reading. Everyone took this work very seriously, and we worked hard at our lessons. Once we mastered the elements of reading, we joined together in groups after work and school to read to one another. Those were the best moments of all.

"Looking back now on what happened during those days, I think that all of us—whether or not we realized it at the time—were desperate to break with the past and establish a new reference for tomorrow. The children, not understanding these things, nonetheless could gain from their elders the feeling of striking out, of breaking free and beginning something new—and more wonderful—in life.

"New families were quick to join us. Soon we were eating better than before, we held a deep-rooted satisfaction of working for ourselves. The slovenly life of the past gave way to a new neatness and cleanliness which made everyone feel fresher and better . . ."

Those were the first memories held by Gherman Titov's father, and they were passed down assiduously to all of his children. By the early 1930s, however, the communes vanished. Stalin's collectivisation decrees abolished the communes, replacing them with the new *kolkhozes* (collective farms), which were based on much of the commune principle, but were greatly extended in their land areas and numbers of people. It was almost as if the communes overnight had expanded to large towns and villages.

Stefan Titov never relinquished his hold on education, and through the years spent night after night in reading and studying. When a new school opened in Polkovnikovo, Stefan Titov became the school's instructor in Russian language and literature—a fact that was to have tremendous bearing on the life of his son, Gherman.

Stefan Titov recalls the early days of Gherman, and his sister, Zemfira: "Gherman's childhood was spartan enough. We four lived for years in a single-room log cabin. I knew every piece of wood in that building, because I had built it myself. Round fir logs sawed in half, piled one atop the other, round sides out. We placed mud and straw in between the logs to cement them together, and then plastered the interior with more mud and straw.

The women smoothed over the interior and dabbed a pastel blue wash against the walls to take away the drab colors. Thank heaven for the windows, for these gave us the feeling of a home instead of simply a room. They were double-insulated windows, and I remember that even as I was putting up the inner panes, the snow already was piling up against the outside.

"Fully half one entire wall was filled by a giant stove, which we whitewashed often to add lightness to the room. The stove served to keep us from freezing to death in the winter. Later, when we built an additional room, we moved small stoves into the second room where Gherman's mother, Alexandra Mikhailovna, prepared for us the wonderful dishes that Gherman remembers so well to now . . ."

This was not all, of course. It is amazing how much living and how much diversity of life may be concentrated in the smallest of living spaces. To believe that people who live in such a fashion, physically isolated with much of the world and, to a great extent, denied during the winter months the communications we accept today for granted . . . to believe that such life demands an intellectual or a social vacuum is wrong.

There is a hard-driving fulfillment of life, a communion with nature that must be experienced to be known. The winters are violent, but they are not always so. There is great beauty, a sweep of life in the mountains, a tingling sparkle in the air, a feeling of oneness with life itself. People share more quickly, more deeply than they do when sated with the physical oddments of life that we know today. Under the circumstances of the Titov family and their neighbors in the communes, and later the collective farms, intense interest is paid to the smaller things of life. Personal relationships are dear to one and all, and a deep sensitivity in social communications creates a rich reservoir of personal reliance. There is no question that a person ever need be alone, except by his own inner whims.

Everything becomes more alive, more alert. A man looks at a

great fir tree weighted down with the heavy fall of snow from the sky, and he sees more—much more, than a tree. He knows his own reliance upon nature, and so he comes to understand better that his is a closed cycle of life. He sees not simply a tree, but a representative of life. He sees nature in its growth. Knowing these things, he is tender and careful with all things growing and all things living. Life is terribly precious under the conditions of Altai in Sibera, and so man and nature come to live closer together.

But it would be wrong to separate the Siberian regions as exclusive of a way of life. It was not so different in any pioneer areas, it is not so different today in such regions as Finland, Alaska, parts of Sweden and of Norway. The relationship to the American frontier regions perhaps is the most meaningful, since it provides to the American a better bridge with which he may gain a better understanding of the type of young life that so markedly shapes a man of the future.

In young Gherman's home, two single iron bedsteads took up about a third of the cabin's space. An oval dining table and chairs were squeezed in between the beds, shoved tightly against the beds, as the latter were against the wall. In one corner a bookcase made by Stefan and his son sagged with books; in the other corner was a cupboard filled with many small items necessary for everyday life.

Gherman's sister, Zemfira, recalls with laughter their sleeping arrangements. "Gherman slept on a shelf above our mother's bed, and I was jammed onto a cot between mother and the stove. Maybe it was Gherman's being tucked up there beneath the ceiling that gave him his first feelings for height . . ."

The people in the small village of Polkovnikovo remember the young Gherman well. Like the other children of his age, when only three years old he was placed on his first pair of skis. But even as a youth he began to stand out among the group. Gherman was a bold lad, inquisitive, ready to try anything that caught his interest. Taught from the beginning that rubbing his body with snow in the winters would protect him against the cold, he quickly became accustomed to the stinging, sharp sensation along his body.

And like many others, school in the summer meant long walks or a bicycle, and in the winter—skis. On his free days, which were none too often, he always turned to his first love—long excursions into the woods to fish and to hunt, a boy close to nature, understanding her ways and her wiles, becoming animal-intelligent himself in a country where wolves still were a danger.

Above all else, the boy Gherman Titov is remembered for his grim tenacity. When he set himself to do a task, he turned to that task with violence, if this were necessary. He flung himself into whatever needed to be done; his was an ardent, absolute surrender to his goal, and he flagged himself on mercilessly to accomplish his goals. This, in turn, gave rise to his weakest point—a hot, black temper that might erupt with startling suddenness. Indeed, Gherman was perhaps overly intense.

Yet, it was this same characteristic that in the future would come to his aid, time and time again. There would be a day when Gherman Titov—not a boy any longer, but a potential cosmonaut to breach the shores beyond this planet—would climb into a fearsome structure called the Chamber of Silence. Here, cut off from the world, deliberately and absolutely rejected by all things earthly, isolated and frozen in silence, Gherman Titiv waited the passing hours, then minutes and, finally, subjected as were other men to the normal rupture of time scales—to the passing of seconds. Other men, many of them stronger than Gherman, could not bear this intense strain. They cracked, shouting and crying out to be released.

Not Gherman . . . and many of his close associates say that they can well imagine the black-haired cosmonaut in that Chamber of Silence, gritting his teeth, and determined to outlast anyone and everyone. And he did.

Gherman Titov's stubbornness manifested itself in many ways;

these were at times detrimental to his official service record, but at the same time the Russians are a stubborn people, and they respect the tenacity of their own. The people of the village in which he was raised are quick to remember incidents that reflect this trait, and they do so with pride. One man recalls driving through a black Siberian night when, suddenly, his headlights illuminated a strange object huddled across the roadway.

The driver slowed his truck and, recognizing the object as a body, screeched to a stop and dashed onto the road. He turned the form over, and gave thanks that the child—it was a young boy—was still alive.

About ten years old, the youngster collapsed from cold and exhaustion. He was so badly frozen he could barely speak. When the truck driver bent down to pick up the child, the lad refused to relinquish his grip on a bundle clenched in his frozen fingers. The driver hauled both the boy and his bundle into his arms, noting with surprise that the old sack clasped by the boy weighed more than the child. Driving back to the village, the boy thawed out sufficiently to gasp his name; Titov. The truck driver took him home. Later that night Stefan Titov explained.

The child was his son, Gherman. He had been standing along the road, hoping for a lift back to the village. When darkness fell without any vehicles passing by, he began to walk home. But the sack he carried was too heavy. Gherman struggled with his burden until he found it impossible to carry the sack any longer. He dropped the sack to the snow, dragging it behind him. Finally his little body could no longer perform even this task, and the boy fainted—bitterly cold and exhausted. He awoke, to begin crawling home, and could not remember when again he lapsed into unconsciousness. The next thing he remembered was looking up at the truck driver.

His father understood, and his pride was great. In the sack was flour—food for the Titov family. The year was 1945, and even as little food as a single sackful of flour could mean the difference between life and death for a family. "It was not only the fact that the flour was precious," explained Stefan Titov. "Gherman had been entrusted to deliver this food to us. He refused to give up, no matter how tired and cold. He would not admit he was beaten. My son would have died that night on the road before that sack could have been taken from his hands."

Gherman Titov was still in elementary school when a new world opened up before him with all the impact of a thunderbolt. As a boy he held a tremendous fascination for anything of a technical nature. Life in his small Siberian village did not permit such an interest to flourish easily; nevertheless, Gherman studied every scrap of paper, every magazine, every book that spoke of mechanical objects, of machines and, above all else, of flying. He made up his mind early; he would become an engineer or, at the very least, should he prove unable to do so, he would become a mechanic.

Until one day . . . when Gherman Titov had a visitor, and through the magic of words and animated descriptions, he turned his gaze upward to the sky. Despite a tendency to be ultraconservative, the author cannot help but comment that young Gherman Titov—like so many great pilots the world over—took his first steps upward, right then and there, in the Altai provinces of Siberia. There are hundreds of pilots who become the greats of flight who can look back upon a moment similar to this one in the life of the Titov boy.

The visitor was Gherman's uncle, returning on military leave to the village. Gherman stared in awe at his uniform—blue tabs and wings, the glittering insignia, but above all, the wings. The boy's eyes opened wide. He had never seen even a town; an airplane was a magical thing that burst across the heavens with an angry snarl at all the world, and then vanished in the unknown reaches beyond the mountains.

And here—right before him, to talk to him!—was a man whose very own world was the sky. A man who had fought in aerial battle against the Germans during the great war, a man who still flew, who could weave his hands through the air and paint for his nephew the sorcery of soaring through the clouds.

His uncle spoke; Gherman listened, enraptured. His uncle spoke of flight; Gherman was hypnotized. His uncle told him of the sun on high, of light glittering off silver metal, of the feeling of power beneath the hand of a man—he spoke of these many things, and a fire grew in the heart of the boy, a fire that was never to die out. His family was to hear this later, in a manner that spoke more eloquently than could any words, of the fierce desire that had been born within the boy, and which he would follow through with all the tenacity for which he was already so well known among his family and friends.

Riding home from school one afternoon on his bicycle, he swerved suddenly to avoid an animal that dashed before him. Gherman tumbled from his bicycle against some rocks; he rose unsteadily to his feet, his face white with the pain of a broken arm. The bone had snapped cleanly just above the wrist. That afternoon a doctor placed the arm in a plaster cast.

But in the next several days, Gherman walked about with a worried and drawn face. His friends had explained that now he could never become a pilot because his arm was certain to become stiff in the plaster.

Unknown to anyone, Gherman each day would sneak off to a nearby lake. Gritting his teeth, he inserted the entire cast into the water to make the plaster soft.

Then, sitting on the lakeshore, his face reflecting the severe pain he suffered, Gherman would begin to exercise the muscles of his broken arm. He would clench and unclench his fist, moving his fingers back and forth. The agony washed through him until several times he retched. He returned home white as a sheet, but brushed aside all questions as to what was causing his obvious pain. Not until someone spotted Gherman doing his arm exercises did his family, or anyone else for that matter, discover what had transpired each day at the lake.

What was to come next could only be a matter of time until Gherman reached the age where he could truly work toward a career in the air. In June of 1953 he completed his schooling in his home village, and several days later applied to the Soviet Military Commission for acceptance as an aviation cadet. Several weeks later, he was delighted to discover in strict medical examinations that his arm presented no problem and—wonder of wonders—he had been accepted as a cadet in an Air Force Training School!

In the fall of 1953, the Titov family escorted the young man to the Ovchinnikov railway station. In his shirt pocket were the official orders that authorized his transport to Kustenai in Northwest Kazakhstan, where he would report for duty to the primary aviation school.

He was superbly equipped for what lay ahead—and little of the future years would be anything less than strenuous and severe. Gherman's health was superb, his school record excellent. The fact that Stefan Titov was the village schoolmaster in Russian and literature had provided Gherman with a broad and deep education. His own aptitude and inclination for mechanics would stand him well in the years to come.

And above all, there was in the young man a streak of stubborness that would drive him forward through all obstacles. It would prove the single greatest ally in the trials that awaited him— trials that were designed and intended to break down his will power. By their failure, they marked the success of Gherman Titov, and they opened wide the stairway up and beyond this planet of man.

And now—Gherman Titov tells his story of ascending that stairway, and of looking down upon this world of ours.

2. Flight

No man ever forgets the first time he leaves the earth beneath his feet, the first moment when the planet falls away, dropping far below. It is a sense of wonder that pilots everywhere have known. It is a oneness among all fliers and, as so many men have stated before me, there is only one first flight to remember. After this, there are moments to recall, to look back upon with feeling and emotion—but only that one *first* flight.

Shortly after I arrived at Kustenai, I marched with an instructor to a training airplane. I did not expect so quickly to fly, but the school believed in their students getting into the air immediately upon reporting. They were here to learn to fly, and that first taste of soaring in the skies would give them a mark by which they could set their personal sights.

I remember little about the airplane, its controls, or the sensations of the flight itself. This contrasts with our conversations that night. The other students spoke with gleaming eyes of how the slightest movement of the control stick brought a frantic response from the wings, and the horizon reeled over in unexpected and, to some, sickening fashion. My own feelings were different. As we rolled down the runway I concentrated for the moment on the bouncing of the machine—its small sensations of shock from the wheels as they jogged over the runway. And then I knew a sensation of speed as we raced low over the ground just prior to taking off. This excited me greatly, for at this moment I was moving faster than I had ever traveled in my entire life. But the impressions were fleeting; there was the blur of the propeller, the whining snarl of the engine, the ground rushing past and then—the flight itself.

I cannot ever tell of the marvelous feeling that swept through me as the earth fell away. The nose of the airplane lifted higher and higher until only the blue of the sky and scattered clouds showed before us. But my gaze moved quickly from here to a greater, more wonderful sight to behold.

Before me stretched for countless miles the steppes of Russia. They swept outward in every direction, virgin land, endless in view, rolling beyond my sight over the visible horizon far from me. We climbed higher and higher, and I paid scant attention to the slight rocking motions of the airplane as we brushed through air currents. A fleeting passage through wisps of white—sharp, hard motions as we lifted above the cloud levels and then I became totally enraptured with the miracle before my eyes.

The rolling steppes drifted everywhere. Small croppings of green that I recognized as forests stood as lonely outposts in the vast stretches of the rolling ocean of land. There was only country to see—mile upon mile of the steppes, and nothing to mar their nakedness. Until this very same year that I began my student training in the air, the great steppes of this part of Russia were, except for some trappers or government explorers, completely left to the wolves.

The airplane banked; I still do not know if the instructor was talking to me at the moment, but if he saw my face, he saw the wonder of it all glowing about me. He turned the airplane gently; the horizon fell over on its side, the nose of the airplane swept swiftly around through space, and more of the panorama lay before me. Now, there was more than empty steppes. I could see the great new wheat fields, harvesters crawling like bugs across them, dragging behind small clouds of dust and wheat that the surface winds rapidly shredded. Great as were these new fields, they were as nothing before the vastness I commanded in those first wonderful moments of introduction to the skies.

The more I thought, later, about that flight, the more I gained that sense of delight about it all. I thought of that strange new perspective of earth and sky, the manner in which a man controls the angle at which his world stands, simply by moving a stick or tramping down smoothly on a rudder pedal. When we landed, I was eager for more of the same—and at once! I wanted to return to the air, and I was overjoyed with the fact that I had hardly yet arrived at the school, and was already aloft.

But this was all—for many more weeks to come. We had tasted the beauty and the awe of it, and then we were brought back with a resounding crash to reality. Shortly after the last trainer skimmed across the grass to land, the cadets reported before the commanding officer's headquarters, lined up in a stiff brace at attention. His words were chilling:

"Comrade students! For the time being you are not going to live here at this airfield. You will all move to another place for your training. You must become accustomed, and at once, without wasting any time, to becoming a military pilot. I stress for you the word *military*. You will build your own quarters. They will be adequate for you, but that is all. Things will be difficult. I wish them to be difficult for you. From your trials and your difficulties you will be able to build your character, to earn your future as military pilots . . ."

I learned quickly that our commanding officer meant every word that he said about life being difficult. Day after day we were thrown at the soil. We were the first cadets at this school, and before we could go to classes and live in even minimal quarters, we had to *build* them ourselves! We dug trenches for latrines, hacked at logs and cut and sized them for buildings, nailed and sawed and hammered and lifted. The days melted into a blur of back-breaking work, of calloused hands, of blisters, of complaining muscles. We were certain to be some of the healthiest and strongest cadets in the Air Force before we ever turned to an airplane.

Some cadets complained bitterly of their assignments. They argued that they had come here to learn to fly, not to dig trenches and to carry logs. But the majority of us voiced no complaints. The sky was too inviting, too wonderful for us to become unhappy about some physical work. And before we realized that several weeks had fled, the initial structures were completed. We moved directly into our ground training.

In much the same respect, we were hurled into studies. From sunup to sundown we studied; we listened in classes and when called upon to answer, our instructors stood for no nonsense. Those who could not meet the rigid standards were quickly informed of the commander's unhappiness over their status, and a second infraction of the most rigid of all rules—a lack of desire to struggle through against all obstacles—resulted in immediate dismissal from the training school.

My attitude here, I suppose, was much the same as it had always been against all problems I'd known before. You do not overcome your obstacles by complaining about them, or searching for excuses in lieu of successes. Years after leaving this primary school, a close friend to whom I had written often presented my wife with the letters he had received—and saved. One letter in particular reflects my thinking at the time better than I can recall, since it was written with the thoughts of the young man *then,* and not in retrospect. The letter was dated April 11, 1954, when I was just eighteen years old.

"... I only came to know Anatoli well in his last class," I wrote. "He has no will power at all; this is a fact and not an impression. And not only because he never entered the military school, but because at any given period in his life, he had failed to cope with the situation that faced him. He did not complete his secondary school, as he should have done, because he was adamant about giving up his personal pleasures. Which means, as I said, that he has no will power. In fact, he never really *wanted* to enter the military school, and only talked about this to make a big impression on his girl friends.

"I just received his letter today. He now is bitterly repenting, and I can just see him beating his breast because of all his philandering in the past.

"... If I do not bore you, let me quote the things my father taught me. Through the years they have proved to be absolutely correct, and even now, when I am meeting really for the first time life as it truly is, I find his words almost prophetic. He has told me, time and again, that work is the most solid basis for life. He taught me to learn to work—that's what makes a real man. It helps him to stand up and to face all his daily problems, and even the worst misfortunes that may overcome him. I remember my father's words, and whenever the going gets rough here in school—as often it does!—they are of great aid and comfort to me.

"And you, my dear friend, are also somehow a bit too despondent. You write almost with tears of your problems when, truly, they are insignificant things. A real man ought always to face up to everything firmly, with conviction; he *must* look his difficulties straight in the face. In a word, study *does* come with difficulty. But really, it's a vital necessity. It seems to me that things are not so bad with you—you're only making them out to be so. Sometimes it happens this way—you persuade yourself that you are ill, and then you really *are* ill. This is what is happening to you now. Take care—and face up to life. It's really not so bad after all! All the best ..."

But in truth, I could not always follow my own advice. In things technical, in terms of training and in flying or in any kind of work, I never knew any problems. If a man perseveres, then obstacles exist only to be destroyed, to be pushed aside, to be eliminated.

As the weeks passed I acquired a deeper knowledge of the air. I learned quickly enough that simply knowing how to fly—in terms of making mechanical movements of the airplane's controls—is a far cry from being a skilled pilot. No man truly flies unless he understands the intimate relationship between his aircraft and the medium of the aerial ocean in which he moves.

Our instruction courses on the ground pounded this knowledge into us, and for myself, this was simply a deeper expression of the fascination I found in engineering and mechanical subjects as a youth. An airplane is a machine, a mechanical device. In the skies its performance is not magic; it reacts to physical forces which a pilot must know, must understand, and must be able to apply to his flight.

I learned all those things that countless pilots had learned before me, about power and lift of the wings and the differential air pressure about the wings that enables a heavy machine to soar through the skies with a performance no bird will ever dream of knowing. I learned to blend mechanical knowledge with the ocean of air. To many of the cadets the rigorous schedule called for much complaining about the constant work; I soaked up everything, and spent my free moments digging for still more knowledge. I was absolutely in love with every moment of the training.

And gradually I progressed through the school to the moment when I would once again return to the air. That first flight upon reaching the school was only a dim memory now, except for the wonder of gazing out upon the vastness of the country. At that time, however, my hands had not touched the controls. Now it would be different. I was no longer a novice, and with all the knowledge that I had absorbed during the long weeks, I would be expected to be able to apply that knowledge with some skill in the air.

Some pilots gain extra fortune in the absolute confidence they hold in their instructors, and in this respect I could not have done better. Pilot-instructor Gonishev, a stocky man with powerful shoulders, flew as do the angels. His blunt hands, strong enough to break the bones of another man's hands, caressed the controls of an airplane with a tenderness that I found both amazing and wonderful.

With my feelings building up toward this initial instruction in the sky, I could hardly have been prepared for what I can only describe as a long anticlimax. My first view of the land from the air had been so marvelous that I could hardly wait to get my hands on the controls of an airplane. Gonishev took me up in a Yakovlev 18, a piston-engine trainer used as a standard instruction aircraft throughout Russia. From the moment the wheels left the ground that flight was nothing but *work*.

I was *not* impressed—I was tired. The only thing I remember about being in the air was that the flight was long, and it was tedious. I did in the air virtually everything I had done on the ground. Gonishev stayed on top of me for every second. There was not a moment's time to relax, to enjoy the skies. It was work, work, work. I kept asking myself when it would end, when we would be back on the ground. As it happened, it almost ended very badly.

We were returning from the air practice area to the field. Gonishev whipped the trainer into the pattern for approach and landing, and finally straightened for his landing. We were just about to touch down—Gonishev had flared out; brought up the airplane's nose to settle down on the main wheels—when suddenly a truck drove directly across our path. The airplane hurtled directly toward the truck in what seemed an inevitable smashup.

In a split-second reaction Gonishev simultaneously rammed the throttle forward and jerked back sharply on the stick. The Yakovlev burst upward in a sudden roar of power, streaking over the truck with only inches to spare. Gonishev climbed back to the pattern altitude and came around again for a landing without incident.

After parking the airplane and cutting all the switches he climbed down from the cockpit, leaned against the wing, and inhaled deeply on a cigarette. "Well, Titov, that's the way it goes sometimes," he said, and walked off to find the truck driver. I was amazed. If these were the kind of lightning reactions a pilot needed in peacetime—at the end of a very dull, routine flight—what must it be like under combat conditions!

From this first flight, I was in the air almost constantly. We trained day after day in the Yak-18 trainers. One after the other the students made their solo flights, gaining that final bit of confidence that is inevitable with the knowledge that, finally, you have flown by yourself. The instructor's seat is empty; there is no one else up there with you. The mistakes you make can no longer be corrected by someone else. You are, truly, at last completely on your own. I must confess that I looked upon the solo flight simply as another step along the road to becoming a pilot in the full sense of the word. I was more anxious to continue flying than content to rest on the laurels of solo flight.

When everyone had soloed, demonstrating their required proficiency in the Yaks, we transferred to a more advanced flight school at Stalingrad. Here we were introduced to the Yak-11, a faster and more maneuverable airplane than the primary trainers. My feeling did not quite match that of the others. They looked eagerly for their flights in the higher-powered Yak-11 trainers, and I felt a stab of disappointment that we were still flying airplanes with piston engines and propellers. I fairly itched to get my hands on a jet fighter.

We saw many of the jets, of course. The beautiful machines, gleaming in the sun, their wings cut sharply back, every now and then screamed over the training areas like some product of aerial sorcery. I looked upon them with an ache in my heart, and almost a frenzied longing to race through the skies in one of these powerful fighters.

If anything, the instructors at the Stalingrad school were even more strict than we had known before. My new instructor, First Lieutenant Lev Maximov, studied me for several minutes, and then snapped: "Above all, *study*. Train yourself *now*, not as a student, but as a fighter pilot. You're going to have to learn how to move without thinking, with instinct. You're going to learn how to use an airplane as a weapon. Get accustomed to speed, maneuverability, to lightning reactions! Second-best is no good here."

I gained my instructor's respect when I was selected as the first student to make a solo flight in the Yak-11. The initial solo was cautious; a routine takeoff, circling the field, and then coming in for a smooth landing. As the training program progressed, I moved into flights that took me to great heights above the countryside, that lasted for more than an hour, and then graduated into aerobatics. First there were steep turns, with the airplane almost standing on its wing.

I was taught to make tight turns of 360 and 720 degrees—through one and two complete circles—and woe to the student who could not keep the nose of his airplane on the horizon, who lost or gained altitude during these turns! Unless we turned so smoothly and neatly that we ran into the vortex of air generated by our own flight —a satisfying *bump!*—as we came about for the second turn, our instructors were greatly displeased.

We learned to loop, and this was a maneuver in which I found great joy—as I did almost all aerobatics. I enjoyed pushing forward on the stick, diving the airplane to build up speed, listening to the increasing whine of the engine and the sound of the wind rushing by. Then, back on the stick, sagging down in the seat from the centrifugal force of the pull-up, and up and up, higher and higher, the horizon and the earth vanishing before the speckled flashing of the clouds. Up and over, upside down, coming back down now, easing off on the power by pulling back gently on the throttle.

"A good one, Gherman, but not good enough! Again, and again!" And again and again I went through the loops, through slow rolls and barrel rolls, the wings swinging around and around, again and again until I could bring the airplane through its rolls with the nose staying right where the instructor demanded it to stay, no dishing out with a sagging drop through the sky. Smoothness and skill and efficiency, and an airplane acting as if it were born to be in the heavens.

We went through split-S maneuvers, Immelmanns, falling leafs, spins, stalls, Cuban Eights, a wide variety and an interplay of maneuver after maneuver. Finally, we were judged well enough in our proficiency to begin flying closer to other airplanes. We learned to fly formation, wings close to one another. We were taught the little tricks of holding the wings level, sliding in and out of formation by using only the rudder pedals with our feet, skidding neatly in and out of assigned blocks of air space off other airplanes. The weeks passed and skill became more and more natural to us.

And then we were ready for mock air battles with our instructors. There are few things so downright effective in cooling off the enthusiasm of a student than such a pastime. The student is alive and joyous with his skill in the air. He has mastered his machine, he is tremendously confident. But all this skill is with an airplane he flies in an air space generally free of other craft, except for the formation work. And then, suddenly, he must pit what he knows and what he can do against the superb touch of the instructors. It is a strange feeling to be so confident, and then have your instructor make you feel as if you are clumsy and irresponsible at the controls!

One morning I had just completed a "battle" with Pilot-instructor Maximov. We were returning to the field to land, when, without warning, Maximov's airplane seemed to burst into being right alongside my own, so close that my heart turned cold. My immediate instinct was to slam down on the rudder pedal and snap the stick over to the side, hurling the airplane away in a flick roll. I was certain that Maximov was about to collide with me. Somehow I clamped down on my feelings, strained not to move so much as a hair off course.

When we landed, I pushed back the canopy and shouted across to Maximov's plane: "Any comment?"

"No!" he called back, grinning. "You're getting the feel of your wings. That's all, Titov."

I was right; Maximov *had* been testing me. It was one of the most effective demonstrations I'd ever received about another required characteristic of the fighter pilot—iron nerves, and the ability to control every reaction, rather than always responding instinctively to a situation that *appears* to be dangerous. Maximov was well known in the training school for his tests of precision—demanding from his student not only skill, but a demonstrated ability to control himself during any kind of situation.

On one occasion, the instructor flew with me for my first extended corkscrew dive—a complicated maneuver in which I was to snap the airplane over into a tight spiral, and keep diving toward the earth. I started into the dive, the wings whirling about madly. Down and down, around and around, the horizon flashing about wildly in a streaked blur of fields and sky, a kaleidoscope of flashing lights and colors as the earth leaped upward at the training plane. I counted the spirals as we plunged—one, two, three, four, five . . .

Now we were so low that buildings and tractors, and people working in the fields, were clearly defined . . . six! . . . and still we plunged. A cold sweat broke out over my body; Maximov all this time had said not a single word. Now the trees stood out clearly, and I swear I could see the leaves! Then the radio crackled and I heard Maximov's voice, crisp and cheerful; "Enough! Pull out!"

I needed no second order. I straightened out the airplane and pulled back hard on the stick. The nose sucked up toward me, the horizon flashed in front of my eyes, and then we were soaring skyward again, easing off on the airplane's speed.

"Titov! Did you feel that seventh spiral?"

"Yes sir! You bet I did!" I called back to Maximov. I licked my lips and dried the perspiration on my hands and forehead.

Maximov laughed with delight. "Well, Titov, you've got the feel of your wings. You can now consider yourself as really starting to be a pilot—you have that special feeling of the seventh spiral. That one separates the men from the boys!"

All my life new things always attracted me, but in this respect I suffered quickly the loss of the eagerness for a new step upward once I had completed the initial work. That first series of spirals in the corkscrew dive were breathtaking. Remembering my re-actions—the cold, clammy feeling; the cold sweat that broke out on my hands and forehead—I went back into the air to repeat the maneuver, again and again and again until I approached, ran through and completed the spirals with little more interest than if I were simply flying straight and level.

When I received the news that our next phase of flight training was parachute jumping—all pilots must learn the technique of jumping before they can earn their wings—I was overjoyed. The thrills there must be in leaping from an airplane, in falling through space—wonderful!

Through my training I constantly applied myself at gymnastics, and in a thousand ways this intensive application paid off hand-somely for me in agility, reaction time, and coordination. An Air Force doctor with whom I discussed my broken arm explained that the only way in which I could assure myself of eliminating all possibility of weakness in the arm was through strict gymnas-tics. From the moment of that conversation, I spent every spare mo-ment in the gym. I worked for hours on the parallel bars, swinging my body around and around, balancing on my hands, going through every exercise possible that would strengthen my arms and especially the arm that had been broken. We had reveille every morning at six o'clock, but for weeks I was awake and dressed at five, running to the gym so I could spend an uninterrupted hour on the parallel bars.

One morning at the Stalingrad school we awoke to find the world blotted out in white. For four days a blizzard raged through the countryside, grounding everyone from flying or even working with the airplanes on the field. By the end of the fourth day a black pall hung over the barracks and classrooms. But then came the message I had been awaiting so anxiously for months. As soon as the storm cleared, we would begin training in jets—in MIG fighters! *Jets!*

As a special token of the training program completed to date, I was provided with a copy of my records in which my instructor, Lieutenant Maximov, and the school's chief instructor, Captain Buivolov, wrote: "Particular attention should be paid to this young trainee. He will develop into a first-class pilot. He flies boldly, confidently."

Those words meant more to me than anything else that happened during all my training. And now, to those long-delayed jet fighters . . .

My instructor for the transition to the MIG's was Captain Valerie Gumennikov, famed throughout the Air Force for his wartime exploits in the air, and an ace many times over against German fighter planes and bombers. But with his war record came a burning passion for discipline in the air and on the ground. Gumennikov stood for no nonsense in the military bearing and smartness of appearance of his cadets, and he set himself up as an example that left absolutely no doubt of what he expected from his students. His uniform was never less than impeccable; his black boots gleamed like mirrors in the sun; his cap was always set at precisely the required angle. He expected—no, he demanded—precisely the same spit-and-polish from his cadets.

This attitude did not always meet with the appreciation from his students, who until this time had been quite content to walk about in loose, comfortable clothing, more relaxing than neat. Gumennikov fairly roared at those people he caught dressed in such fashion, and the day when two students appeared in his classroom with gym togs resulted in an explosion from the captain.

He ordered them to their feet and in a brace at strict attention. "I know what you think," he grated at them in acid tones, "but I will have no pigs in *my* school. Let me warn you straight off. Don't delude yourselves with your sloppy dress, because it only reflects on your sloppy attitude toward your flying. If you possess an inner sense of neatness and precision, if you keep your things tidy and squared away on the ground—then you will maintain these same characteristics in the air. Discipline is necessary at *all* times, in the air and on the ground. And in jet fighters discipline is tantamount to survival. Sloppiness in these machines will not be tolerated—not by me or any other officer—by the airplanes themselves. They will reward your conduct in this fashion by killing you. And I care more about losing airplanes through stupidity than for your feelings about your comfort. Now, leave this room at once, and do not return until you can present yourself in the manner that a future officer should. Get out!"

Gumennikov ended his problems right then and there.

If my first training flight in the Yakovlev airplane left me unimpressed, my reaction to the jet fighter was exactly opposite. I will always remember those incredible and wonderful moments.

From the very first I felt a tremendous impression of speed. That first flight in the Yakovlev was so long that at the time I was anxious to return to the ground. But this! I lined the MIG up on the runway, ready for takeoff, holding the airplane steady with the brakes. Then I advanced the throttle in a steady, careful movement. When the engine produced its maximum power, I lifted my feet from the brake pedals. The fighter lunged forward to race down the runway.

I was awed by the beauty of it all. No propeller turning before me . . . no engine thrashing and pounding . . . no banging vibration from the airplane. The fighter sped straight and true down the runway, accelerating with tremendous speed. It was a simple matter keeping the nose pointing down the runway; the jet engine produced no problems of torque as I had known in the past, when I had to press down hard on the rudder pedal to keep the airplane from swinging off the runway.

In what seemed to be barely seconds the needle read more than 150 miles per hour, and I eased back ever so slightly on the stick.

It wasn't a takeoff; the earth simply vanished beneath the wheels of the airplane. Immediately I hit the switch to retract the gear, and swing into a wide, climbing turn to circle the field. Gumennikov sat quietly in the airplane with me, saying not a word, leaving me entirely to myself. I had just enough time to circle the field, to drop the gear and the flaps, and line up for the landing. The fighter settled down like a feather, the wheels kissing the ground with a faint sigh. That was my first jet flight—and my first true flying.

I found that Gumennikov's famous discipline was even stricter in the air than on the ground. He was more than severe when it came to flying; he was a fanatic for precision, for discipline, for perfection. The standards of other instructors meant absolutely nothing to him. Sloppiness in the air was certain to produce a black rage from this man, who wanted *his* students to be the best in the Air Force. It was not enough for a cadet to complete a good training flight simply by adhering to his requirements of flying a selected altitude, course, and speed.

When one flew with Gumennikov, one had to produce surgical precision in flight. Every move was either made with a precision that blended science and art, or the instructor's wrath would descend with scathing condemnations upon the student. With this man I truly loved to fly. He set standards which I could and did appreciate. Gumennikov was almost brutal in his insistence upon quality, and I was stubborn enough to want what he, and he alone, could give to me. He made his wants clearly known, and it was strictly up to the student to meet his requirements. The man who could do so was certain to become an excellent pilot.

Finally Gumennikov decided it was time for me to graduate to my next phase in training. I was assigned to a new instructor— Captain Stanislav Korotokov. And with the new assignment came a special honor. The bulletin board placed my name at the head of the list of all cadets—and I was given the honor as the first student to solo a jet fighter. I received this news with a deep satisfaction at having applied myself so completely to my flying.

Needless to say, that first solo flight was everything it was supposed to be. I took to the skies that day with all the sensations of flight and the wonder of the heavens that any one man can possess. It was one of the most satisfying moments of my life.

But near disaster to my flying career followed almost immediately behind the event. During certain occasions in the past, I had run afoul of my own temper. I was too quick with outraged reaction, too young to appreciate the need to bend to the military system, too brash to recognize a requirement for tact with my anger. At a special meeting I was stung by the caustic remarks of a colonel, with whom I had disagreed. Instead of speaking in terms which reflected military courtesy, I shouted back at the officer, adding certain remarks which were incredibly foolish for any cadet.

The colonel apparently had a temper even worse than mine, and he fairly exploded on the spot. The difference in our tempers was that I was the cadet—and he was the colonel. He shot to his feet and demanded the strictest of punishment to be inflicted upon me at once—which could have meant an immediate end to my flying career. I had committed an unspeakable sin of military protocol, and this man demanded—and by virtue of his rank, could get— maximum punishment.

I have Captain Korotokov to thank for saving that career—and everything else that has happened in the ensuing years. A man of tact and extremely cool bearing, he turned to the colonel.

"I dare say, sir, that I know young Titov as well as anyone in this room," he said. "It is true that he is at times overly obstinate in his views. But it is equally as true that his crime essentially is one of the brashness of youth. Perhaps he has not yet had sufficient time to realize that as a future officer who is to give orders, he must learn to accept orders—pleasant or not—and to carry them out instantly. His fault at the moment is in slighting authority, but this is not deliberate. It is his reaction when he firmly believes he is right, and this is his manner—wrong or not—of simply trying to make his point."

The captain then leaned back in his chair; he had his audience, and now he used every bit of his tact to defend me. "We have to watch Titov for his tendency to extremes. But why should we punish him just because he defends his point of view? Is this not what we want from our future pilots? You cannot convince a man by shouting at him. Nor should you try.

"You must prove your point. You must do it with reasoning and sense. There are so many positive things in Titov's character; his sober independence of thought, his will power, his discipline in every other respect, his superb flying ability, his creativeness. These things are too good to be thrown away; we must cultivate these and not simply root them out because of this one tendency. We shall control this . . ."

I was embarrassed at the captain's words. Fortunately, the other officers in the room supported his statement, and the colonel whom I had offended withdrew his demand for a court martial and punishment. But no matter what relief I felt, it was a close—and a dangerous—call.

Later that day, Korotkov drew me aside. "Titov, you are an ass," he ground out between clenched teeth. "Have faith in yourself. That's good. But have faith in others, too! Not blind faith, but tempering with reason. You were wrong in there today, and you are a fortunate young man to have gotten away with that stupid temper of yours . . ."

From this moment on, I made every attempt, and was successful, in curbing my temper. I realized just how closely I had come to destroying everything which I had worked so long and so hard to create. And things went more smoothly for it all.

Finally the course reached its conclusion. There were the final examinations, the final tests in the air. I was overjoyed with my record. From theoretical to practical studies, in the areas of precision flying, target shooting, aerial combat maneuvers—I read a string of "Excellent" comments after the subjects. And then I stood with all the other students as the results were read aloud to the entire school. I was embarrassed at this public attention—but no less delighted with it all.

On my 22nd birthday, I read the order signed by the Minister of Defense, Marshall Zhukov, that ended my training as a cadet. From that moment on I was a lieutenant of the Soviet Air Force, ready for duty assignment—and immediately I requested service with a combat squadron.

I was very proud of the wings on my uniform.

3. Tamara

My life was full. Each day I took to the air as a full-fledged jet fighter pilot of the Air Force. Daily I rose into the skies on swept-back wings, propelled through the thin air of high altitude by a powerful jet engine that blazed with fire, yet gave me only a whispered rush through the upper reaches of earth. There is a miracle to flight when you sit in the cockpit of a fighter . . . the world is open and clean; through the curving plexiglas nothing interfers with vision. The airplane is a product almost of sorcery. A pilot's head is insulated within his helmet and earphones. With his radio turned off, even the slight crackle of radio static is gone, and the machine seems to ghost through the skies. It is wonderful to command such energy and flight. It is as flawless as flight may be, and I enjoyed every moment above the earth.

But I am in error, to be truthful, when I remark that I was fully a jet fighter pilot. I had won my wings; that was true. But my education had only begun. I was now able, so to speak, to learn the most essential elements of the life of the fighter pilot. Being able to fly, no matter how well, is a far cry from understanding the intricate nature of mass operations. Combat flying today is not simply a matter of rushing out with bravado to engage the enemy. It demands a coordination of men and machines in the sky, linked electronically to ground command stations, woven together with the invisible fabric of radar and radio. To blend all these into a smooth operating force is a task difficult to accomplish. While I flew, my edge as an operational pilot was still to be honed. Nonetheless, every moment spent in the process was sheer joy to me.

There was much more to learn than the sharpening of my abilities in the air, and as a member of a closely coordinated aerial team. Now that I had left behind my days as a student and a cadet, I enjoyed the privileges of a commissioned officer in the Air Force. I imagine that the social life of an Air Force officer here is much the same as anywhere else in the world, and perhaps there are also additional advantages. The Soviet Air Force enjoys the highest respect of our people. There are advantages both direct and indirect in terms of allowances, pay, travel, and the like. Air Force officers are much in demand at social events, and it was no secret to any of us that a young Air Force officer was not at all disliked.

Unhappily, this did not afford me—personally—any advantage. In all other things I believed problems existed only to be solved. But where I would accept a challenge in any area of which I could conceive—when it came to the opposite sex my tongue immediately became tied into a knot, my feet stumbled awkwardly and, to my eternal embarrassment, even a pleasant conversation would turn my face a beet red in color.

This was so painfully obvious to my comrades that what was originally cause for derision soon became matter-of-fact. No longer was my absence at the beginning of dances or parties a cause for special comment, and it became accepted that I would usually arrive quite late and leave as early as possible. While present at the party, I was certain to be found in a corner of the room, earnestly discussing flying or anything else to do with flight. *Anything*—so that I might avoid the unpleasantness of shifting like an idiot from one foot to another before a woman.

Until one early evening in the spring of 1958. Whatever the occasion I do not remember, except that several hundred pilots and their dates were all having a wonderful time at a social dance. Lying on my bed, furiously intent on a book—I remember that on this evening I was deep into H. G. Wells—I glanced at my watch. The party had been under way for more than two hours. Dislike as I did joining the others, I was expected to act as an officer—and that meant the social amenities as well.

I put off the obvious as long as possible by writing a long letter to my parents. Then even that was done. I dressed, put on my cap, and walked to the dance hall. I was in luck; at the far end of the room several pilots were hard at it, and their hands waving in the air supplied evidence of an intense flying discussion under way. I hurried to join them.

I never did discover the exact nature of their animated conversation. A girl stood between myself and their group. I was about to pass her when she smiled; I stared . . . I *knew* this girl. The old shyness swept over me, but I could not just keep walking by her. She was still smiling, and in my tongue-tied desperation I asked her if she would dance.

I remember, next, only moving across the floor, brushing by the other couples. I remember . . . a waltz, a flashing smile, dark hair . . . and her name. Tamara.

When the music began anew I looked at her, and then at the dance floor. She nodded, and once more we danced. And again and again. Wonder of wonders, I was enjoying myself! When I avoided talking for fear of stumbling over my words, she did not force the conversation. When I did speak to her, Tamara's easy answers and ready smile melted away all the confusion I had always known.

She was fascinating; a beautiful girl of the Ukraine. Her eyes glowed in the soft light, and her laughter was soft, yet deep. When I spoke of flying, I was amazed not to hear the trivia that such a subject invariably brought forth with a woman. She only nodded at times, but her comments revealed her knowledge of aircraft and of the Air Force.

"Tamara . . . why is your face so familiar? I *know* I have seen you before . . ."

She laughed, and shook her head to deny me the answer. "On the airfield," was all she would say. For the life of me I could not place her . . .

It really did not matter, for time fled without my awareness of its passing. The moon glowed close to the horizon when finally I took her home; we had danced for hours! We agreed to meet the next evening, and I was startled to see how easily, how quickly, I assured our next time together. Her parting words failed to dismiss my conviction that we had already met. "If you look carefully, Gherman," she smiled, "you may see me before the night."

The next morning my inquiries at the breakfast table about Tamara brought forth the inevitable laughter and jokes of my finally having danced with a girl. And more than once! Each time I asked about her the other pilots grinned and replied only with a question. "Your breakfast all right, Gherman?" Were they all crazy? "It's fine, it's fine . . . what is the matter with all of you?"

A captain roared in glee. "It should be, my fine young lieutenant," he shouted. "*She* cooked it for you!"

Of course! I went to the kitchen immediately, and there was Tamara, in white apron and cap . . . she, of all people, was the unit cook. "Good morning, Tamara!" I called. Her teeth flashed in a smile.

From this first meeting, we were inseparable. I had found in Tamara the wonder of life in a vein I did not know existed and, of course, could never know without her. Tamara stripped away from my life the shell that stood between myself and the deep rivers of emotion we would soon share.

There really was no courtship. We came together as if only the moment of meeting was the catalyst needed for two people. In every possible instance we joined one another, walking for many miles in the fields, allowing the growing love we found for one another to open our eyes to nature, to life, to the intensity of sharing things.

Fortunately, we could spend much time together in our work. Camp movies, lectures, meetings . . . we eliminated effectively the barriers of time and work that separated most young couples.

No one questioned, least of all us, what became taken for granted. From our first evening, Tamara accepted no dates with any other man. It was unspoken, for certainly I could never have asked this of her. We just . . . accepted our togetherness.

Two months after we met, I asked Tamara if she would be my wife.

Our wedding ceremony took place quietly, a moment that we both cherish and look back upon fondly. With us were several immediate friends, my regimental commander and his deputy, and a new-found friend—my instructor, Squadron Commander Shulyatnikov.

Our new life came to us as easily as turning the page of a book. Everyone helped us to begin our married life, and the regimental commander surprised us with the best gift of all—an apartment right on the airfield itself. We might have lacked for room, but as small as was the apartment, it proved no less a blessing to us. Many a night it shook to the laughter and the happy words of our friends. It was my first—and a wonderful—home with Tamara.

Each day, each week and month, opened my eyes to the tremendous diversity of life, of new emotions. In my flying, and my wife, I was indeed a happy man. I knew the conflicting emotions of looking forward eagerly to each flight, and yet, anxious to return as quickly as I could to Tamara. And with her, content in a manner I had never before known, I still felt that deep, inner tug from the skies above. Nothing could have been more wonderful for me.

Yet we were host to an intruder. I discovered the problem only slowly; the evidence lacked substance enough for me to understand a note of dissension. Tamara was—had been from the moment we first met—nervous about my flying. What was subdued completely in the intensity of our coming to know one another revealed itself in the more quiet moments of our marriage.

It was not that I flew badly; Shulyatnikov rated me as one of his best pilots. Tamara also knew this. Her concern was that I flew at all. From some moment or incident in her past of which I knew nothing, Tamara held an intrinsic dread of the skies.

Her feelings disturbed me, and I tried to convince myself that the passing of time would allay her fears. They did not, and as the months passed, my concern grew. All pilot's wives, I imagine, suffer the fear that gnawed at Tamara . . . a fear she tried bravely to disguise, but could not. The other wives either accepted and lived with their concern, or pushed it away from immediate awareness in their marriage.

Unable to do this, Tamara became openly upset about my flying. When storms or fog grounded our fighters, her delight was both astonishing and intense. She bubbled over with sudden happiness; she could not do enough for me to fill the hours I spent on the ground.

But when, for whatever reason there might have been, my fighter was overdue from a mission, Tamara suffered a succession of black moments melting into a continuous nightmare. Every time a jet's distant sound cut through the night, every time a whisper drifted down from the clouds, Tamara would awaken, fearful that it might not be . . . my airplane.

She could not simply wait, as other wives discovered finally that they must. More and more frequently she responded to long flights or missions when we were overdue by making worried telephone calls to the regimental commander. Or else Tamara would in her anxiety call our operations room, asking the inevitable questions of where I was at that moment, when would I return, was I safe . . .

Her concern, personally, was dear to me. I worried for Tamara, and yet there was no choice but to tell her, as gently as possible, that she must discontinue her calls. There is an unwritten law among our Air Force, as there is with the men and women of every air force throughout the world, that this is something a wife simply does not do. You do not call and voice your concern. Your worries are real and intense and they are hateful; they gnaw and they grow. But a woman must live with them, as Tamara in time came to do.

But only in respect to the outside world. Never did she relinquish within herself that deep, emotional fear. I discovered this one night on my return from an unusually long mission. I came home to our apartment to find Tamara asleep at our kitchen table, her head cradled uncomfortably in her arms.

She awoke with a start, so relieved to see me that tears showed on her cheeks. "Oh, Gherman," she sighed, "forgive me . . . I did not mean to go to sleep. I hate sleeping when you're up there . . ."

Things have long been different. I do not know whether Tamara still looks upon the skies as her enemy. But now, of course, it may seem even to her that the ocean of air about us is a warm, sentient thing compared to that vastness beyond.

Never will I forget an evening in the fall of 1957 . . . an evening in October. That night I stood alone on the airstrip at Leningrad. It was a flier's night, an evening that belonged to us who make the heavens their home. A brilliant full moon cast a silvery gleam across the metal of the airplanes, and the stars hung in the sky with a hard blue light. Far across the airfield, moving into the gentle night breeze, a jet fighter flamed its way toward a nocturnal rendezvous. The airplane itself could not be seen, but I traced its movement by the blazing gem of orange light from its tailpipe, a light that ascended magically away from the earth. It rose gently but swiftly away from the horizon, shrinking in intensity and size until the stars opened wide to swallow the color and the light itself. A faint whisper of thunder from its passing drifted by on the breeze, and then it was again silent.

But my gaze was riveted to the heavens. There—a shooting star! A sudden movement of light amidst the stars themselves, it seemed.

But no . . . almost at the same moment I knew this could not be so. The light was too crisp and clean, a light that looked like a star itself, but without the flashing facets of those distant suns. It could not be Venus or Jupiter; it was *moving*.

It could not be a star, I knew. It was too bright now, too close to be in the heavens. And it failed to burn out, so it could not be a meteor.

I could not understand what I saw as my eyes followed the light, moving rapidly across the background of stars. It must be the light of an aircraft, high, very high above the earth.

Even this, however, could not be true, for if that light came from an airplane—what a fantastic machine that must be! To move as rapidly as it did at what was obviously a great height, why—the airplane had to fly with a speed three or four times that of sound. And no one flew *that* fast.

I stood transfixed, watching the light disappear slowly into the stars, fading with distance. Frowning, displeased with myself for my inability to identify immediately what I had seen, I returned to my quarters. Several hours passed before I could sleep.

The next morning I knew beyond question the wonder of what I had been so fortunate to see. That light in the sky was not among the stars, and it was not a machine flown by a man through the atmosphere.

It was a light where there had never before been the light of man. When the first excited cries came across the field in the morning, then I knew I had seen the first satellite ever sent into orbit about this planet.

The light in the heavens was our first Sputnik . . . and never could I have imagined that my own reach above the earth would in only several years' time bring me to the heights of that first satellite.

If Tamara could, then, have known what was coming, I believe that she would have given everything to have kept me in my beloved jets. But, of course, neither one of us could forecast the miracle of tomorrow that was yet to come.

It was years away, but the door opened soon afterward.

4. Assignment for Space

Low clouds and ground fog swept low over the countryside, spilling down valleys into Leningrad and sweeping across our airfield. With the other pilots of my squadron, we looked gloomily out the windows of our operations office. High above the racing scud, storm clouds loomed miles above the earth. Our prospects for flight this day were almost nil.

Someone called my name; standing in the door was the deputy to the base commander. Beyond him I could see his car, the door open and the motor running. "Titov! Come here—and don't waste any time, man; the commander wants you in his office immediately." I climbed into the car, and the driver took off in a wild spray of mud and water. I sat back, silent; what on earth could prompt such special attention? It was ridiculous to ponder what I could not know, so I sat back, my mind a blank. I would know soon enough.

During the next hour my confusion mounted rapidly. An Air Force colonel awaited me; with him was a lieutenant colonel of the medical service. You do not ask brash questions of colonels—I had learned *that* lesson well!—and so I replied as quickly and as effectively as I could to a running barrage of questions.

What did I think about jet fighters? What about their speed; fast enough? Did I know what experimental fighters were in the process of development . . . what did I know, how did I feel about speeds many times that of sound? My heart quickened when I heard these words. Many times the speed of sound! But only for a moment could I dwell on any particular point. The two officers continued their questions, staccato, one after the other, probing for something.

The conversation drifted from airplanes to their propulsion; propulsion in turn drifted, as inevitably it must when you discuss great speeds, to rockets. Was I interested in rockets? In rocketry? Had I kept up on the latest developments in rocket science and use; I had.

The questions ended as if someone had thrown a light switch. The colonel lit a cigarette and leaned back in his chair. He stared at me, his gaze hard and piercing.

"There is a new field of aviation about to open up, Lieutenant Titov," he said slowly. "We want men who are willing to undergo special training. It will be extraordinarily difficult, and likely it will also be dangerous. You are one of a very select few who are being offered this opportunity."

He blew out a great cloud of smoke. "But first, Lieutenant, you must understand that I mean exactly what I say when I describe this training as arduous. It will be back-breaking. It will go on day and night until it drives you crazy. Understand all these things. Now, then . . ." he paused. "This is the opportunity you are being offered. The offer is made, as of now."

I requested permission to think the matter over. The colonel rose impatiently to his feet, grinding out his cigarette beneath his boot. "There is no time to think anything over, Titov. Once again I ask; are you interested?"

I stood up and snapped, "Yes, sir—I am!" All of a sudden the nature of our discussion crashed into my brain with the impact of a bullet. He had been talking about much more than rockets— several times he had used the term *spaceships*. But to me, such things were still dreams for a distant tomorrow.

Sputniks were one thing, carrying as they did instruments, or even a dog. But a spaceship . . . to carry *men*? The thought was dizzying. The colonel nodded his pleasure, and left immediately with his medical officer. They told me to return to my normal schedule of flight; I would be notified soon. But I had no idea of exactly what the notification would be for, where I would go, what I might be called upon to do. It did not matter; all I could think of was that magic word, *spaceships* . . .

I arrived home with my feet barely on the ground. I knew I could not repeat the conversation to Tamara; especially when she greeted me with the joyous cry that we were going to have our first child. That night I told Tamara only that I would be taking some special flight training that might well result in a promotion for me. Tamara scarcely heard what I said—the prospect of the baby occupied almost all her thinking, and temporarily at least it banished her immediate fears of my flying.

Several weeks later I received orders to report to a nearby hospital for an extensive medical examination. Still I said nothing to Tamara, and she had not the slightest notion that when I kissed her goodbye, I was leaving on my first step for a selection course for . . . space!

At the hospital I waited in a large room with dozens of other pilots. I noticed we were all approximately of the same age, we were all pilots, and we had yet one other common denominator; every man was an excellent physical specimen. With the group were several senior officers from the medical corps, working with scientists and technicians. From almost our first day at the hospital we were placed on a dizzying schedule.

Through the confusion and the endless tests and examinations the impact of what I was doing slowly took root in my brain. Rockets, spaceships, cosmonauts . . . it was almost too much to believe. We were, really, told very little by the people who examined and questioned us. This was not so much a matter of secrecy, for all of us had been informed as to why we were present; it was a matter of a lack of criteria.

What is the best type of man for a cosmonaut? No one knew,

of course, since such a need had never before existed. Our discussions among ourselves sometimes appeared to reach the height of absurdity, since conjecture ran riot and imagination enjoyed free rein.

The qualifications for a man to hurtle through space—we knew from the start that the goal of the new program was nothing less than manned orbital flight—could accurately be determined only with experience. But such experience simply did not exist. Some of the pilots insisted that a spaceman should be tall, that he would need great muscular strength; others who were informed on the engineering problems laughed at this, saying that the problems of weight dictated a smaller man. Then there would come a voice that spoke with authority, ending such arguments with the crisp words that weight presented absolutely no problem to us, that we had the rockets to send a dozen men aloft. The problem was simple enough; the man had to be skilled and he had to be tough, he must be a superb pilot, an engineer, a navigator, an astronomer. The more we heard the calm words on the requirements involved, the more we feared for our individual chances ever to see any more of the program than the hospital in which we were being examined.

But there seemed no question that whatever men were selected, their first criteria was to be superb health and physical fitness. Looking around at the other men with me, moving with all the smooth balance and agility of a cat, I said a silent thank you to that doctor who had prompted my extensive workouts in the gym. Perhaps that broken arm I suffered as a boy might prove to be a blessing in disguise.

Hardly was a man silently thankful for his own physical condition when the psychologists struck with all the force of a battering ram. Their questions became an endless drone, and I recognized soon enough that the more irritating queries were designed specifically to incite me to anger. And they were good at this, too, as I caught myself just in time—more than once—from lashing back in kind. Finally it became impossible for me to make rhyme or reason from the questions, dashing as they did from one subject, one mood to something almost alien in nature.

Afterward the physiologists and psychologists decided upon those men who would continue in the competition and those who would be spared any further torment, by the simple process of being dropped out at once.

We did learn more, in terms of scientific requirements, of the size of the men most in demand. The project scientists explained their needs to us as a combination of a man who was highly intelligent; able to grasp clearly all the technicalities of the flight; capable of the highest mathematics and many general sciences; a skilled pilot of many years flying; a man of extensive experience; a man too young to have gained extensive experience; strong enough to withstand crushing physical punishment from gravity forces; and, after all this, small and light enough not to require too many of the scientists' valuable cubic inches of cabin space. "In other words, gentlemen," one scientist said gravely, "all we want is a quart in a pint pot." The potential cosmonauts roared with laughter.

Even from the start we each recognized the unpleasant fact that the Air Force had assembled far more candidates than were to be accepted. This fact, however, only increased the severe competition. As the days wore on and we were provided with more and more information of what the future held, our imagination soared as though it were rocket-propelled. "The cosmos itself . . ." We almost whispered the words in awe. And the more we learned of the enormous rockets being prepared to send men into space, the more intense became our determination to do our best in the many examinations.

In the rare free hours between the endless inspections, questioning and lectures, we took advantage of a large wooded area near the hospital to relax. Under the tall pines we fished, read, or simply spent our time discussing the wonders that the more fortunate among us would one day come to know.

We had good reason to look upon that "one day" as not being too distant in the future. Every one of us read every scrap of information on our satellite and booster programs to date. I recalled clearly that night when I stood on the Leningrad flight line and watched Sputnik I race in its ghostly silence across the heavens. We crammed into our heads every last iota of information on the flight of Sputnik II; the fact that for a week the dog Laika had suffered no apparent ill effects from her prolonged weightlessness afforded us all good cheer.

But the chief topic of our space conversation was the most recent satellite—Sputnik III, which raced into orbit on May 15, 1958. Our first two satellites had been impressive, but the 184.3 pound payload of Sputnik I, and even the 1,120 pounds payload of the second sputnik, remained far from even minimum requirements for a manned space flight. Sputnik III was another matter entirely. The complete second stage thundered into orbit along with its heavy payload, and it was exciting to imagine that ponderous vehicle racing around the planet in the vacuum of the cosmos.

The satellite itself was big enough to contain a man and the equipment necessary for his support in space. Sputnik III was nearly twelve feet long and six feet in diameter, but most important was the vital fact that the satellite payload weighed 2,925 pounds. The second-stage rocket booster, orbiting about the earth, measured more than eighty feet in length. All the statistics were impressive to us; the conical satellite raced from its perigee of 135 miles in a wide, swooping orbit out to 1,167 miles beyond the surface of our world. And the speed! Sputnik III shot through space with a velocity of 18,837 miles per hour as it passed close to the planet. Right there—a *fact* in the heavens—was the rocket and the container that, technically, could carry a man away from the world.*

* The Sputnik III satellite orbited the earth for 692 days, re-entering the atmosphere on April 6, 1960. The booster orbited for 202 days, re-entering on December 3, 1958.

We computed with slide rules the additional payload weight possible if the engineers restricted the satellite to a low earth orbit of about 100 to 110 miles at the perigee, and no more than 160 miles for the apogee, or high point of the orbit. In this type of orbiting maneuver, the speed requirements for orbit dropped by a thousand miles per hour—and the payload weight increased accordingly. So a manned flight would certainly soon be feasible. But first they had to find the man . . .

Each week our ranks thinned as the severe medical examinations dictated their casualties from among the hopefuls. The centrifuge especially exacted a heavy toll. In this instrument a man climbed into a special seat, much like that of a fighter airplane. Technicians strapped him down securely. In the earlier tests he had only to sit still and absorb the battering that high centrifugal forces imposed upon him. Later, he was required to operate airplane-type controls as the centrifuge whirled around and around, faster and faster, until the man strapped into the seat began to sag beneath the punishing forces of many times normal gravity. Six, eight, then ten and twelve and even higher G-forces; a man's limbs became lead and his blood thundered in his ears until, finally, flesh and blood no longer could sustain consciousness and the man lapsed into a welcoming world of blackness.

We lived, it seemed, for fully a week in different pressure chambers. We donned pressure suits and helmets, and sat uncomfortably in steel tanks as engineers sealed the tank, and then with a great roaring gasp exhausted most of the air inside the chamber. We worked and ran through special tests under simulated space-environment conditions. We shot to high altitude in seconds, and plunged down as quickly. We took off our masks in thin air to determine our resistance to hypoxia—to lack of oxygen. We sat impatiently as we were subjected to explosive decompression, a sudden and sometimes violent reduction in the chamber pressure, that had the equivalent effect of rocketing a man in a fraction of a second from low altitude to many miles above the earth.

We ran on treadmills, hopped up and down on first one foot and then the other, stuck our feet in ice water until our teeth chattered and we seemed to turn blue. We breathed into tubes for scientists to study every detail of our respiration. We shivered in cold chambers and perspired profusely in other rooms where blazing lights turned the room into a seeming inferno. We allowed wires to be attached to our bodies, and then twitched like frogs in a laboratory when the wires came alive with electrical current. The doctors examined, probed, studied, questioned, tested and did everything but dissect us, it seemed!

The most vivid memory I have of the tests was the "vibration seat," a devilish affair that almost drove a man to distraction. It was hardly an impressive device, since it was nothing more than the front bench of an old, broken-down bus. But engineers had modified its drive shaft with an engine that produced the wildest vibrations I have ever known. Under full throttle the engine whipped the seat into a paroxysm of vibration that rattled a man's eyes in their sockets. After several seconds the seat was almost unbearable, and even breathing became impossible.

"To the cosmos—by bus!" became a sour joke among us, for word spread quickly about the acute discomfort afforded by this local transportation line that never went everywhere. I came to know these devices all too well; in the next two years I repeated many times those same tests that, at present, were used simply to obtain a hard core of the most qualified men among us.

But, for now, the doctors and scientists were intent only upon rooting out the basic weaknesses in the potential cosmonauts. They succeeded too well with me, I fear, for near the end of the experimental course my patience had reached the thinness of a razor blade. All this time I prided myself on my ability to outlast the others, or to stand shoulder to shoulder with the best of the men competing with me. But as the days stretched into weeks, I came to hate the constant proddings and pokings of the devilish machines the scientists had devised. I began to grumble to myself, and came to insist that much of the "torture" was totally unnecessary. Rather than simply relaxing in my mind and accepting whatever discomforts were being applied deliberately to me, I began to lash out. And one day I almost went all the way out of the competition, a move that would have been my eternal sorrow.

One afternoon a psychologist asked me—for the hundredth time within an hour, it seemed—how I felt. I snapped at him. "The sooner I can get out of here, the better!" I said sharply.

The doctor looked up at me, and I should have read in his raised eyebrows and heightened interest the warning signs that were there, clearly to see. "Oh? Why," he asked quietly, "can't you stand the competition?"

"It's not that at all," I said through clenched teeth. "But this is ridiculous! I'm a healthy man, I have no problems, and I seem to be doing nothing here but wasting my time answering a lot of your silly questions."

"Silly questions?"

"Yes!" I retorted. "I cannot see the point in many of them. And you and your associates ask them interminably—over and over again. All I want to know is—am I fit, or not? Let us get this stupidity over with once and for all . . ."

The psychologist stared at me with eyes that were suddenly steel-hard. "That—your fitness—is precisely what we are trying to determine." He threw his pencil down on his desk and for several seconds glared at me.

"Lieutenant, there are different standards of fitness," he continued. "The man who goes into space will be among the most spectacularly capable of men. He must face a whole new horizon of hazards. Some of them we know, but these, bad as they are, do not concern us. The unknown hazards are the real problem, and they demand the very best if they are to be overcome. The man we elect to send away from this planet will need tremendous reserves of energy and strength . . ."

He warmed to his subject, pausing only to stab his finger at me.

"That man will have, perhaps for the sake of his very life, a sharp eye and a clear brain, or he will never be in the ship that makes those early flights. He will, because he must, be unafraid of what lies out there beyond this atmosphere about us—" he waved an arm over his head to accent his point—"and we must know that he can cope with anything. That's *anything,* young man, and I mean precisely what I say.

"Our standards of fitness are like none that have ever existed before. Our methods belong entirely to us, created for this particular purpose. Everything we do has a purpose in mind; nothing goes on here with you or your colleagues that has not been carefully planned and predicted. We cannot afford mistakes."

I must have looked startled, because he raised his hand to prevent interruption. "With rockets we can make mistakes. That is permissible; that is the science. But with men—never! So there is no room, my young lieutenant, in this program for anyone who feels that such precautions, no matter how exhaustive, are unnecessary."

His voice was scathing. "Or silly, I might add."

A cold hand clamped around my heart. Right then and there I knew that I was walking the finest of lines. My brash words— would I ever learn to curb that temper!—had almost closed the door to me on the most wonderful adventure any man could possibly know. And for all I did know, I *was* out.

From that instant on—I apologized calmly to the doctor, and explained that I recognized more clearly from his words the intent and purpose of what was happening—I never made the same mistake again. That little lecture, delivered for my benefit when the doctor could just as easily have written a rejection notice on my papers, was a true blessing for me. I came to understand better not only the staggering problems that the technical staff faced in their work, but more important, I gained insight to their methods. And the more I looked upon the tests from this new perspective of mine, the more I came to appreciate the devilish ingenuity and the lengths to which they had gone to probe my mind as well as my body.

No longer did I *resent* the selection program. Instead, each new test became a personal challenge. I accepted the fact that men had devised the test with the express purpose of breaking me down. I had a challenger now, defined clearly and specifically before me. The enemy stood out in stark relief, and with this sort of problem I could come to grips.

The more I probed into myself to find assistance in withstanding the psychological shocks that rained down upon us, the greater clarity I gained in observing changes in many of the other men— changes of character, in attitude, and an outlook on life itself. One of those men, I must admit, was . . . myself.

But my impatience, buried but not eliminated altogether, was yet to suffer its severest test. One morning I awoke with a cold. My nose ran and for a while I sneezed repeatedly. But it was, after all, just a cold. I had had colds before, and undoubtedly I would have many more in the years to come.

The doctors, however, seemed to go insane. They ordered me into a hospital ward and assigned me to a bed as though I had come down with some exotic disease that might run rampant. My temperature rose to a hundred degrees, but what was this to cause so much concern?

For four days the doctors kept me restricted to my bed, while I fumed in helpless rage. I asked to be returned to the selection tests; they shook their heads. When I shouted that I was perfectly all right and could take anything they had to offer, they only looked at me without comment.

Then I was told that I could leave. I dressed quickly and almost ran to the commandant's office where—in shocked disbelief—I was informed that the rest of my course was canceled. My orders were to return at once to my regiment.

I could hardly believe what I heard. How could I have failed? Where did I go wrong? The one incident with the psychologist could not possibly be the failure . . . I knew that the competition was the sharpest in all the country, but I knew also that I had done well. In a black mood, I cursed my rash words with the psychologist and then I cursed myself for having come down with a stupid cold.

Before I left I asked, almost hopelessly, about the results of my tests. An aide replied, "We will let you know later." He handed me my general service papers, and with that sterile gesture I was dismissed.

No—not yet. No one left the program without one final lecture. A stocky, powerful man in civilian clothes spoke to me in a closed room.

"Lieutenant, when you leave this area, you will do so with the absolute knowledge that no one—and I mean absolutely *no* one— must ever learn of what you did here. Your tests, your training, your activities—must remain only your information. You will not discuss it with your fellow pilots, your commander, your wife, or with anyone at all.

"Our project to send men into space is of the highest secrecy to the State. You will regard it as such. You are a possible participant in this adventure, and you must be especially careful to watch every word.

"From this moment on, I want you to think of your activities here as relating only to the latest developments in supersonic fighters. That is your story if you are questioned on your absence. Do you understand this clearly?"

"Yes, sir," I said.

"Good. Dismissed."

That was that. No mention of rockets. No mention of space. And not the barest hint of men in space.

I returned to my regiment, dismayed to find Tamara in ill health. The baby brought on unpredictable moods of despondency. In the weeks following, whenever our flying schedule permitted, I took her on short leaves to Leningrad and twice all the way to Moscow.

But I could not simply forget the incredible promise of those weeks when I had competed with the finest pilots and engineers of all the Soviet. Impatiently I telephoned my squadron commander, but each time my call produced only the same answer. No messages. My own mood grew black. I was convinced now that I had failed, that I had destroyed my own chances.

I returned to our apartment one night with Tamara, startled to see a long buff envelope lying on the floor, where a courier had slipped it beneath my door. My heart quickened as I tore open the paper, but my hopes flagged again when I saw that it was only a summons to report to Moscow. Yet, even this was better than an immediate and irrevocable rejection.

I was on the first plane that left for the city and the cosmonaut training program offices.

There, an officer told me that my candidacy had been no better than a question mark. A man who could not control his temper was not the best selection for a task that could well demand infinite patience under the worst possible circumstances.

"But," the officer paused, "there is something here in your favor. You have been especially recommended by Dr. Eugene Alexeevitch, who is one of our top medical scientists in the program— and, also, a member of the selection board . . ."

I could hardly believe what I heard. Recommended by Alexeevitch? Wonderful! I am *in*; I'd made it!

Almost I heard the words of the officer in a daze. " . . . will report at once for an accelerated series of tests, and you will maintain complete silence outside of the training area."

For more weeks I was run through the psychological and physiological mazes, reacting as I supposed to react, withstanding physical punishment until I could barely stand, while the doctors stared at me with raised eyebrows. I was too tired to even care about their thoughts.

The tests reached their end. For three days batteries of doctors and engineers queried me. Questions, questions, hundreds and hundreds of questions.

And, finally, in stunned disbelief, a doctor grinned, leaned across the desk and shook my hand. His associate clapped me on the back in congratulations.

I had my new assignment—and it might well be the depths of space beyond this world of men.

I walked on air, aided by a deep and fierce pride within myself. But I had to come back to earth; I was given permission to return home, to tell Tamara.

5. The Training Begins

That same night, while a blinding snowstorm isolated our airfield from the rest of the world, I broke the news to my wife. I could hardly keep the secret to myself any longer; Tamara knew instinctively of something strange in the long weeks now behind us. My prolonged absences without explanation of any kind—save the lukewarm story of training for new supersonic jets—had raised more than one set of eyebrows among the pilots and their wives. Tamara was cognizant—without comment on her part—of my deep preoccupation with my secret activities. But to her the proof of the unusual was the fact that for many weeks my swift jet fighter had remained on the ground, its cockpit empty, while I traveled in my ill-disguised secrecy to and from Moscow.

Because the cosmonaut candidates would be in training for months and perhaps several years, Moscow granted permission for our families to join us in new quarters at the training school. I did my best to break the news to her gently. I explained that something special—very wonderful—had happened to me. And to set the mood properly I withdrew from my coat pocket a bottle of wine purchased in Moscow and brought home for celebration.

Tamara's eyes brightened. "Gera . . . a promotion?"

I shook my head.

"A transfer to a new squadron, then."

Again I shook my head. "No, Tamara; that wouldn't be much

cause for celebration . . . at least not until we found out what the
new assignment would be. No; it is something else."

She gestured impatiently. "Gera! Stop teasing me! Will you
please get it over with and tell me what is going on?"

I asked her to sit beside me on the couch. I still did not quite
know how to explain.

"Tamara, imagine a night when there are no clouds, when there
is no moon. A night when the sky is filled completely . . . filled
only with stars. A night when the heavens are bursting with billions upon billions of stars . . ."

She stared at me; I did not return the gaze, but kept on talking.

"Imagine this, Tamara. Imagine the wonder of it all . . . the
cosmos itself beyond this world. Imagine a ship up there; a ship
racing away from the earth . . . moving through space."

I turned and looked directly at her. "Imagine all this, Tamara,"
I said softly, "and, then . . . well, imagine that the man inside that
ship was . . . your husband."

She stared at me in disbelief. "A—a spaceship? A *spaceship?*
And . . . *you* . . ." Her voice trailed off as she leaned back, unable
to talk.

"Yes. Really . . . me."

"You're not serious, Gera, are you?"

I looked directly into her eyes. "Yes, I am deadly serious."

For several minutes Tamara remained silent.

"And you think, Gera, that this is cause for celebration? That I
should be overjoyed at such news?" Her voice was a hoarse
whisper.

The bottle of wine embarrassed me; it felt hot and uncomfort-
able in my hands. Slowly I placed it on the floor.

"Well . . . yes; yes, I do, Tamara," I said in as serious a voice as
I command. "It is the most wonderful news I have ever received,
the most wonderful thing that has ever happened to me. I can still
hardly believe it . . . believe that I was picked as one of the rare,
fortunate few who have a chance.

"You have no idea how important this is . . . what it means to me."

She started to talk, and before a word came, I knew what I would hear. About the child stirring within her, of course; *our* child. This was now Tamara's world, and it was mine as well. She had not yet spoken a word, but I could read in her eyes all the words there were to say. The hours while her heart squeezed in pain when I was long overdue on missions; the times when she feared that she would never again see me by her side, the pain of anxiety and worry; the knowledge that the sky had been, was now, always would be her enemy.

And now *this* . . . this impossible beyond. The cosmos to Tamara could not yet be defined in her terms as they were clinically in my mind. To my wife the space beyond this world was alien, incomprehensible, but yet real and terrible. She could not understand this new danger in a form and shape that was to her describable, but Tamara shivered suddenly as if the cold of space had descended into the room.

I did not allow the words to come. "Tamara, you must understand. This is really what I want. I *must* do this . . . I—no, I cannot explain it in words. Not now, perhaps not tomorrow, perhaps never. But I *must* . . ."

She reached out with her hand, her fingers gently touching my cheek. She said nothing for a long, timeless moment. Then she sighed, and a trace of a smile crossed her face. "All right, Gera," she whispered, "all right."

I clasped her to me, my heart thudding in my chest. Tamara would say not a single word of complaint, there would be not one sound of unhappiness. I knew that now, and I was grateful.

She drew away, laughing suddenly as she picked up the bottle of wine and held it aloft. "We will drink a toast to your tomorrow, after all! Tell me, Gera; when does all this begin?"

I took two glasses from the cupboard, held them out for her to fill with the dark, red liquid. I touched my glass to hers.

"Tomorrow," I said. "The first thing tomorrow morning."

Tamara, startled, looked around the room, at the furniture she had so carefully collected for us. "And all this . . ."

"Leave it; forget about it. Just one suitcase, they said. Everything will be provided for us in the new place."

She raised her eyes to mine, and we drank our toast—to the long tomorrow to come.

During the weeks that my chances for selection as a cosmonaut grew, I had spent many hours thinking of the training that I would receive for a flight through space. My imagination ran riot with all manner of meticulous detail. In my mind I pictured my arrival at an enormous cosmodrome, living and training in spartan quarters, and then traveling to an enormous hangar in which there would stand, gleaming and brilliant, several giant spaceships.

First I would ride a smooth, noiseless elevator hundreds of feet above the earth. I pictured myself stooping slightly to enter the rounded entrance port, staring in wonder at the banks of controls and instruments. I would listen intently as a scientist explained to me the function of each piece of equipment.

As though I looked through a magic mirror to the future, I saw myself in a vast lecture room, walled by charts of the heavens. The voices of scientists echoed slightly as they intoned to me the courses through the cosmos that I would follow, the wonder that was to be mine.

All this I imagined, in some miraculous atmosphere of scientific beauty, of serenity, while everyone looked out upon the cosmos. Ah, but it was a picture to make the hearts of poets tighten and to bring tears down upon their cheeks . . .

The bubble burst the morning that Tamara and I left the squadron for my new life. The great hangars, the gleaming spaceships, the star charts and the shining instruments vanished as though a switch had closed in my mind and banished with some embarrassment my daydreams. My feet were still planted firmly on the ground—and yet I was billions of miles out into space. The first thing I needed to do was to come down to earth.

I did—with a resounding crash.

The day broke cold, overcast and damp, perfectly miserable. A sergeant led us to our new home—a small and pleasant house, but impersonal and cold to us after the first home of our marriage. I left Tamara immediately, my eyes showing their disbelief as I followed the sergeant past a long row of perfectly ordinary barracks. The sergeant explained that these buildings comprised our training quarters.

These? Why, they were the same as any barracks on any training field in Russia! Was this to be the start of that great adventure into the cosmos? Then I had no time to ponder on the vast gulf that separated my imagination from reality, and from this instant on I never permitted myself the foolish luxury of such nonsense.

Our instructors wasted not a moment. I reported to the commanding officer, submitted my records, and went through the same familiar routine I knew from past experience in other training camps. Next, we—the cosmonauts—were introduced to one another.

Every man showed the same kind of cautious reserve; cordial and pleasant, but slightly withdrawn—as I was myself. They were all young, all pilots, all commissioned officers. I restricted my remarks to the polite conversation of introductions.

Even when we made our initial tour of all training facilities, I clamped a firm control upon a tendency to burst out with dozens of questions.

Could this possibly be all there was to a training camp for the new cosmonauts? Was this the beginning to space—barracks, a drill field, and vast open spaces beyond? I warmed immediately to an impressive, beautifully equipped gymnasium, but where was the spaceship? Where were the giant rockets, the launching platforms? Where was *anything?*

Throughout the entire area there existed not a shred of evidence to connect our training camp even remotely with a drive to rush out into the space beyond our world. We might as well have moved into a training camp for the Olympic Games, for the area was filled with gymnastic and athletic equipment—jumping pits, vaulting horses, obstacle courses, running tracks, and tennis courts. What were we to do—lift the spaceship away from the earth by muscle? I was astounded; then disappointed. But I had learned my lessons well.

Keep your mouth shut—and wait. I did exactly that, and it was just as well. Our training began officially the next morning, and I was speechless to comment. ·

At six o'clock sharp, the sky streaked a leaden gray with the first signs of dawn, I paraded on the freezing drill ground with fifty other men. We wore only shorts and a sleeveless shirt, and the cold sliced sharply into our skin.

Our first instructor appeared—bubbling with energy, bouncy, broad as an ox and from the sight of his rippling muscles, every bit as strong. He strode with disdain to the center of the field, glared at us and then roared in a bull-like voice.

"Attention! Right off," he bellowed, "single file, ten paces between each man! When I say off, start running—and I mean *running!* Now—*off!"*

We broke into a trot around the field, unenthusiastic, dragging our feet. A stentorian roar howled over us with all the force of an artillery piece: "I said *run,* dammit; *run!* You walk like old ladies. *Run!"·*

My heart sank. Space training—hah! My feet pounded against the asphalt of the drill field, the cold stung my flesh, and my mind revolted against our now frantic pace. What a way to get to the stars!

"Hey, *you!* Number Five! Yes, dammit, *you!"* I jerked my head around, startled; *I* was Number Five. "Pick up your feet, Five; that's it—*run!"*

I ran. For the next hour, we all ran, chests pounding for air, sweat pouring down our bodies, while the athletic instructor stood in our center, bellowing happily. It was quite a beginning.

In all things athletic, I excelled among the cosmonauts—that is, except for one. Running. I hated to run; I do not know why, but it was an idiosyncrasy I could not shake. My instructors were frantic, for on the drill field I remained the butt of jeers and roaring gibes from our instructor—while in the gymnasium the instructors pointed me out as the outstanding gymnast.

The senior instructor drew me aside one day. "Titov, what's behind your dislike for running?" he asked.

"Everyone has his likes and dislikes . . ."

"And you, Titov, don't like running."

"Frankly, no sir, I don't."

"That's all right," he thundered in his cheery manner. He slapped me with a monstrous hand on the back. "You'll get to like it, lieutenant, you'll get to like it fine!"

Irritated, I snapped back at him. "You can't force me to like it."

He grinned at me. "All right, my fledgling spaceman, it's time to ask you some questions," he said. "Now, tell me, what do you think these things are for? What does running give you, for example?"

The answer was obvious. "Why, it's been explained to us a thousand times. The same things as the rest of the athletics—muscle toning and coordination."

The instructor shook his head in the manner of a wise old bear. "But you are wrong!" he shouted. "You have forgotten the most important thing of all.

"*Rhythm!* That is the key to it, my young friend—rhythm. Running, and only running, develops the feeling of rhythm in the work of your heart and your whole body. You are going to need perfect coordination of muscles and reflexes that you didn't even know you had. And you can get these things only by running, and running the right way."

I ran—for hundreds of miles, it seemed. I ran with my legs

pounding into the cinders below, moving almost by their own accord. My legs and my arms worked in a wonderful coordination, my lungs labored in a precise manner, my heart knew none of the pounding that followed my first weeks at the training camp. I could run for mile after mile, moving almost effortlessly, and I came to know in detail exactly what the instructor had taken the pains to explain—that my body knew a coordination and rhythm I did not believe possible. With my extensive work in gymnastics, I felt as if I could enter the Olympics and compete with the best athletes in the world.

We *all* felt that way. After two months of grueling, constant athletic work, of obstacles courses over which we were prodded again and again until we raced nimbly over obstacles that once defied our best efforts, the men who remained in the training camp were considered the outstanding physical specimens in all the Soviet. Our numbers were less; the increasing medical examinations continued to thin our ranks as the doctors raised higher and higher their severe minimum requirements.

The most nerve-wracking aspect of the intensive physical training was this steady "weeding out" process. After our first two months in the camp we were no longer bothered by whatever athletics our instructors called upon us to do. Nothing they could devise proved beyond our immediate, skillful doing. And the more the instructors failed in their attempts to tax our abilities, the happier they became. Their failure was a sure sign of our success— and that was exactly their job.

But is failed to soften the unexpected sight of another empty chair or a locker from which all clothing and nameplates had been removed—concrete evidence that the doctors were still tightening their standards. It was impossible to predict who might be next, for the doctors judged by reasons that seemed to lack all reality. The slightest sign of a slow reflex, a memory that a doctor considered less than photographic, the barest indication of resentment at the program—any one of these or a hundred other insignificant items was sufficient to reveal to us another empty locker, and another name removed from the list of hopefuls.

As the number of survivors dwindled, we were startled to note almost a parental level of care from our doctors. No longer did they or anyone else find it necessary to prove their point; those still remaining were the elite, and it was foolish to deny that we recognized our own abilities. They changed their attitude of violent competition—in the medical sense—to caution. We went onto the football field with special padding on our bodies; the doctors sitting on the sidelines dashed onto the field to attend immediately to any minor injuries.

My favorite competitive sport was hockey; I loved the flashing speed and counterplays of the game, and soon became team captain. I enjoyed nothing more than racing in toward the goal, whizzing the puck into the net despite the frantic efforts of the goalkeeper to avoid the score. Yuri Gagarin and I became fast friends soon after we met; we played opposite one another on the hockey arena, but joined forces on the basketball courts. And every now and then Gagarin and I would look at American picture magazines and sigh with envy . . . at the wonderful height of the Harlem Globetrotters. Imagine playing basketball when you're seven feet tall!

A marked change in our training began during the middle of December 1960. There were only twelve of us left now, twelve men who were told—in official terms—that we were the outstanding men for the job in all the Air Force. From this point on the physical training of the past several months was over. Except for the routine exercises and sports to maintain our peak physical proficiency, athletic training as such was now completed. From this point on, we would begin the hard technical training of the program. We were, so to speak, at long last getting down to the nuts and bolts of our assignment as cosmonauts.

For several weeks we sat through endless hours of lectures. Scientists, astronomers, technicians, engineers, doctors and other instructors appeared before us on a constant, unbroken schedule. No attempt was made to insure that we were not being overtaxed. The rule was a simple and fitting one: if we were still here, we were the best. If we were the best, then each day would be filled to the utmost with training, training, and more of the same.

We knew by now the name of the spaceship that one among us would be first selected to fly—Vostok. Even the title of the craft sent a deep feeling running through us. No longer were we only speculative of the ship that would be the first to carry man through the void around his world. Our information at first left much to be desired in the way of details, but we were given to understand that as our training program progressed, the essential features of the Vostok would be integrated within our work. In this fashion the spaceship would acquire a special meaning and purpose for us, rather than sitting as an entity unto itself, separate and useless until we were ready to give a ground-chained spacecraft its true purpose beyond our world.

The bulletin board one night carried a notice that we would leave the training camp the following morning for a special exercise. We shouted in jubilation. This could only mean a visit to the technical center to see the Vostok! We talked for hours into the night, discussing the spacecraft, trying to anticipate its every detail.

At the crack of dawn we mustered outside the operations room, eager to begin the day. But in a dispassionate voice our chief instructor shattered our dreams of seeing Vostok so soon. Our assignment for the day—parachute jumping! As part of our physical training we had gone through extensive tumbling, jumping off high ladders, swinging through the air on parachute harnesses suspended beneath cables—the many techniques designed to teach us the proper manner of striking the ground when descending beneath a parachute.

Jumping was familiar to us. All pilots of the Soviet Air Force must be qualified parachutists, but only to the extent of knowing basic procedures and making several jumps. Those pilots on operational duty who so wished could continue to jump, with a bonus for so many jumps made per month—and our Air Force was filled with thousands of men who abandoned their cockpits regularly to leap from transports.

Dispirited at the news that our first sight of the spaceship would have to wait, we climbed into trucks and drove to a nearby airfield. On the snow-covered runway there awaited a large and lumbering Ilyushin transport, ready to take us aloft. We put on our parachutes and climbed aboard. Thirty minutes later out we went, dropping through the large door, falling freely for several seconds, and then yanking the D-rings to release the parachutes.

Two hours later we went up again! And once more this same day—three parachute jumps, no nonsense about wanting to jump or not, on our first day of this phase of training.

That night our instructor made it clear that jump training was only beginning. We were not to be merely qualified jumpers—we were to be experts. All the next day we received extensive instruction in jumping and landing techniques that none of us had ever known.

Each man made several tests in a large hangar aboard an ejection-seat trainer. A fighter-plane seat mounted on rails that led almost vertically upward was armed with a powerful cannon shell beneath the seat—exactly as were our own fighters. The pilot strapped himself down, the instructor counted down his numbers and—*WHAM!* the next instant you hurtled upward toward the hangar roof, convinced you were going to tear right on through. But the seat always stopped as planned—to our relief!

We jumped from different types of aircraft. We leaped out of transports wriggled away from liaison planes, dropped through hatches of other aircraft. We made low jumps, medium-altitude jumps, and then dropped from many miles above the earth. Again and again we went out of airplanes. Our instructors were merciless. We did not complain, but we *did* question the necessity. We were told, clearly and succinctly, that it might prove necessary for us to re-enter the earth's atmosphere at any point below our orbit. "Since it may prove impossible for your gentlement to select the most comfortable place to descend," the chief instructor stated, "you must be prepared to land safely—anywhere—under any conditions."

He made good his point. The next morning the Ilyushin transport took off in a heavy rain, and at six thousand feet out we went, falling through the clouds. In the poor visibility we could hardly see the ground until we were almost onto the surface.

We jumped into trees, on hillsides, into lakes and rivers. We fell into marshes and onto hard ground. We landed in wheat fields and on concrete surfaces.

We made several jumps from fighter planes. The two-seat jets were modified with a separating fore-and-aft canopy. In the front seat the pilot remained within his canopy as we initiated our own sequence. Feet in stirrups, knees tight against the footrests, head firmly back in the cupped metal protector, hands gripping the side rests, then—*squeeze*. First the canopy exploded away. The cockpit filled with a constant blasting roar, but there was hardly time to notice this. A tremendous foot crashed into the bottom of the seat as the explosive charge fired and we went hurtling upward from the fighter, tumbling slowly as the wind whipped about the seat. Then, separation from the seat, a fall for several seconds, and the *smack!* of the harness as the main parachute boomed open.

That was the first phase of ejection-seat flight testing. We also ejected from the fighters while they were in vertical banks, in order better to simulate the angle with which we might leave the spacecraft in an emergency as it descended through the atmosphere.

The parachute jumps were, very frankly, extremely hard on us. Not because of the jumping itself or the parachute drops, but from the impacts against the ground. Bad enough to land in a high surface wind—but to drop in this same wind, carrying a man rapidly over the ground—into trees, brambles, and hillsides, was a painful process! Several of the men sported severe bruises and not a few suffered skin lacerations. To their complaints as the doctors patched them up our instructors replied coldly, "The fault, comrades, is yours. Next time you will pay more careful attention to what we teach you." And that ended the complaints.

To me the worst—and the most dangerous—of all the parachute jumps were the extended free falls. The long free fall introduced a new danger to our training. Fortunately, the hundreds of men who had jumped from very high altitude were able to warn us of the invisible killer in the sky—the dreaded flat spin.

The Air Force spared nothing to give us the best in instruction. Our chief parachute instructor was Nikolai Konstantinovitch, who held several world records, including his most spectacular—a jump and free fall descent for a total of more than 47,000 feet! We listened intently to his every word as he warned us that the flat spin could not be anticipated, could not be prevented from happening. Several men had died from its effects, as the spin gripped them in a deadly web of centrifugal force.

It was just my luck to avoid the flat spin, but to be caught in what some instructors call its "bad cousin." I left a transport as it cruised through a thin, cold atmosphere. Seconds later I jerked the rip cord and the parachute began to spill out. Perhaps I was not falling quickly enough, or the slip stream from the great propellers had whirled me about wildly. Whatever the reason, the parachute and shroud lines drifted out lazily instead of pulling all the way. The next thing I knew I was in a violent corkscrew, the world a terrible blur, flashing around and around. My face was down, my body twisted.

The next few seconds terrified me. I tried to pull out of the violent whirling motion, but could not. My limbs seemed frozen, and then alarm bells clamored loudly in my brain as my head seemed to become heavier and heavier. The world began to turn gray, then darker, and I realized I was close to blacking out completely.

Through a haze of pain I recalled every word of instruction.

With all my strength I drew myself into as tight a ball as possible, clasping my knees to my body with my arms. I gave a convulsive gasp and threw out my legs and arms suddenly, just as a skater will stop a spin on ice by throwing out his limbs. It worked!

Not very well, but it worked. I crashed to the ground still somewhat snarled in my harness, but I walked away from the landing —and that is always a *good* parachute jump.

That evening in the mess the pilots greeted me with a giant cartoon of myself—my legs spread wide, the parachute tangled around my ears, and my collapsing on the ground in an ungainly heap. The caption beneath the cartoon read: *"The Tumbler."* For weeks the name stuck to me, understandable since we were already known to other airmen, in their confusion of our real purpose, as "The Circus."

Nevertheless, I was a proud officer when, with my close friend Yuri Gagarin, we were called from the ranks of the cosmonauts to be officially awarded with the classification of *Parachute Instructor*. It was doubly a good day; at the same ceremony the school commandant presented me with my first official medal of the Soviet Union—*Master of Sport*.

With the conclusion of our parachute training, the technical and classroom studies began in deadly earnest. By the time we completed our bio-cosmonautics studies, every man knew thoroughly the many strange effects upon his body of speed, centrifugal force, acceleration, lack of oxygen, cosmic radiation and all the other forces embraced by the science and practice of cosmic flight.

As pilots we understood clearly that a man ascending from the earth quickly runs out of breathable atmosphere. But what to us had been essentially academic knowledge now gained a meaningful purpose. We came to know almost every page of our textbooks and manuals; we understood the intricate process deep within our lungs of the body's exchange of gases between the alveoli, the blood stream, and the other tissues involved in this wonder always going on within our systems. The road to space became for me a series of plateaus; on each new level an additional requirement came into being—requirements for one hundred percent oxygen, for partial pressure breathing, for full pressure breathing, for an enclosed life-cycle system. I—and the others—could tell in detail almost to the instant when bubbles began to form in the tissues and the bloodstream because of decreasing atmospheric pressure. We studied models, anatomical cutaways, watched films and looked at slides, read and listened until we knew every detail of what happens when the unpressurized lungs are exposed to outside air at a height of fifty thousand feet—a startling and grim process where a man drowns in the carbon dioxide and water vapor in his lungs, which refuse admittance to oxygen. And why, of course, he must have help in the form of oxygen, pressure, warmth, cooling when necessary . . . he must have all these things and more if he is to remain not merely functional, but alive.

We received the equivalent of a broad-base medical indoctrination, with the grim exception to the average course being that we were attempting to learn what would happen to *us*. We all knew the forces of gravity. As fighter pilots, every one of us had experienced the bone-squeezing force of many times normal gravity as we clawed around in tight maneuvers through the sky. We knew, to some extent, the feelings of weightlessness, as our supersonic machines cut swiftly through the heavens, soaring up and over in carefully planned and precisely executed parabolas, balancing out neatly the opposing forces of gravity and centrifugal force. We studied special films showing how the blood pools in the different extremities of the body during fluid shifts imposed by these gravity forces.

I came to know things about my body—and the effects upon it of flight in the atmosphere and beyond—that I never dreamed could possibly happen. More important, we were actually beginning to integrate the capabilities and limitations of the human being's body and brain, with the same extent of capabilities of the robot and machine systems. This was necessary, because this is exactly what flight through the cosmos demands; a strange and wonderful blending of the two. Our lessons taught us the intrinsic key to flight beyond the planet of man: No man ever truly leaves the earth. This is impossible. To survive in that bitterly alien environment beyond our world, he must take with him the most precious and essential items of life that earth provides. When he does so, he can survive. If he fails to duplicate to their minimum standards the conditions of life on earth, the verdict is a simple one. He will die.

Nothing proved more exciting to me in these phases of basic and then advanced instruction than the unprecedented films of actual space flights to date. Since we must necessarily coordinate our activities from the moment of launch with our boost and flight vehicles, we studied thousands of feet of film of our giant rockets ascending from the earth. Each film became blended with technical lectures, until the mass ratio and pounds-thrust of these vehicles became as familiar to us as was aerodynamic lift or angle of attack in reference to our jet fighters.

The films continued, adding starring roles to their stories. The "stars" were dogs, insects, plants, guinea pigs, rats and other animals. Above all, the dogs gained our closest attention as we watched films of the animals during the flights of rockets to many hundreds of miles above the earth. The rockets hurtled far beyond the atmosphere of the earth. From the moment the blazing motors shut down, the rocket and its pressurized containers were weightless. And for many minutes the dogs experienced the actual effects of flight in space.

We watched the films of the dogs, and we felt a growing closeness to that great beyond. We understood dogs, and we could understand what was happening to them. Above all we learned quickly that, aside from the powerful gravity overloads, to which we were already accustomed, the worst discomfort of the flights for the animals stemmed mainly from their confinement in a small space, subjected to the ear-shattering thunder of the rocket motors. This too, proved encouraging, for knowledge of the noise invariably strips away its effectiveness as a problem.

But what brought us to grip our seats in anticipation were the films of the dogs in orbit, relayed to the ground by television cameras as the giant satellites flashed silently overhead through vacuum. We watched the films of Laika, the animal that rocketed in orbit in November of 1957. The transmission of these films left much to be desired. We were not disappointed in terms of improved quality of the films, which came to us from two later satellite flights—one of them proved so successful that we could watch clear, full-color films of the dogs in orbit and under conditions of prolonged weightlessness.

On May 15, 1960, Russia hurled into orbit the heaviest satellite to date, known to the world as Sputnik IV. To use this name was strictly for statistical charts—the satellite was to us the single most important space achievement to date.

Sputnik IV was actually our Spacecraft I. The satellite was the first step in our program for manned flight, which called for the successful orbiting and safe return to earth of at least three separate Vostok-type spaceships. Spacecraft I began the actual in-space program.

From every point of view, the spacecraft was impressive. First, it followed the natural line of division of our cosmic rocket program. In October and November of 1957 we launched the first two Sputniks. Then, in May 1958, Sputnik III with its heavy 2,925-pound payload raced through space at nearly 19,000 miles per hour.

Our scientists devoted the year 1959 almost exclusively to our program to probe the moon. We all had followed with intense interest the flight of Lunik I, which left the earth on January 2 of that year. Our first deep-space probe, weighing just short of eight hundred pounds and followed by the third-stage carrier rocket (which itself, without fuel, weighed 3,246 pounds), shot past the moon at a pass-distance from the surface of only 3,200 miles. That was a tremendously satisfying shot, especially after the much-heralded but unsuccessful series of rockets that the Americans had fired in their launchings to the moon.

Impressive as was this first cosmic rocket into deep space, the following two giants held far more importance to us because of their critical guidance requirements. On September 12th, Lunik II burst away from earth's gravity with a velocity of 24,950 miles per hour. Success or failure depended entirely upon how precise our scientists could be in their allowable launching error—our orientation on these flights emphasized that if we experienced an error greater than only *one second*—against a burn-out velocity of about 37,000 feet per second—we could miss the moon.

We roared with joy when the results came in. Shortly after burn out, we received the word that the tracking stations were predicting an impact on the moon about thirty-five hours after power was cut off. Thirty hours later they revised this estimate, and the tracking gear showed that they were only 84 seconds off schedule for a flight lasting thirty-five hours and covering a distance of nearly a quarter-million miles. In celebration our instructors hung a giant map of the moon in the mess hall, with a large red star showing the point of impact—only 270 miles from the center of the moon.

Our third and final moon rocket for 1959 left the earth only three weeks later, on October 4th—another good cause for celebrating, since the firing date was exactly two years to the day after Sputnik I ushered all men into the new cosmic age. And again the reports we studied accented the tremendous skill and ability of our rocket and electronics scientists. Lunik III eased past the moon, its total weight of more than two tons separated into the photographic satellite as one component, and an additional 343 pounds of instruments left with the carrier rocket, which soared far out into space before returning to the earth. There is little need here to review the spectacular success of Lunik III, and its historical photographs of the other side of the moon—an area which we hope one day to visit in person.

After the moon rocket program in 1959, our scientists felt they had accumulated the background, experience, and equipment necessary to begin in earnest our manned space effort. The first evidence of that new program came in the form of Spacecraft I, a manned satellite that went into orbit with a "dummy cosmonaut" aboard. The guidance equipment worked beautifully, hurling the 10,008-pound spaceship into a near-circular orbit around the world 188.5 miles high. It was—and still is—one of the most perfect orbits ever achieved.

But the flight did not achieve full success. After four days in orbit, our scientists sent an electronic signal to the spaceship. Inside the spacecraft was a pressure cabin that weighed 5,512 pounds, and the final goal of the flight was to fire a small rocket that would separate this compartment, slow it down in orbit, and bring it back safely to the earth's surface.

Something failed out there in space. The pressure cabin separated successfully from the main spaceship. Small stabilization jets then flashed in the vacuum. Unfortunately the automatic system did not properly orient the pressure cabin. The retro-rockets fired in the wrong direction. Instead of re-entering, Spacecraft I actually moved into another orbit three miles higher than before.

The scientists did not consider the failure to be critical. This was our first spacecraft in the series, and the first test in space of the new retro-fire and re-entry system.

But where the first spacecraft attempt in its final phase encountered failure, the launching on August 19th of Spacecraft II was successful beyond all the scientists' wildest dreams. The heavy satellite, virtually a duplicate of the Vostok in which we would one day fly, weighed over five tons. In the spacious interior were two dogs, as well as containers holding rats, mice, flies, fungi, plants, seeds, and several television cameras.

The firing was perfect. Spacecraft II whirled into an orbit with a height ranging from 189 to 210 miles, and then began a series of experiments within the cabin that provided the cosmonauts with many hours of fascinating films. Watching the animals as they floated about under zero gravity, their bodies completely weightless, entranced us. For hour after hour we studied the films televised down from space—and were then afforded the sharper clarity of color films taken by automatic cameras within Spacecraft II.

For where the first of the manned-type ships failed to return safely to earth, not so Spacecraft II. More than twenty-five hours after the five-ton craft rushed into orbit, the command signal flashed from the ground into space. Retro-rockets blazed in vacuum, and the heavy spaceship decelerated sharply. Soon afterward it began its plunge back into the atmosphere, operating perfectly under automatic control. It came to earth beneath its huge parachutes after completing eighteen orbits in space—a flight of 437,500 miles.

No other single step forward proved so exciting, so rewarding or so vital to our manned space program than did the flight of Spacecraft II. With this spectacular success behind us, the last doubts as to our rocket and spaceship systems for manned flight vanished. From this point on, our scientists needed only to perfect advanced types of equipment.

They made their next firing on December 1, 1960. Spacecraft III shot into orbit, again with a weight of more than five tons. And again the spaceship was an unmanned predecessor of the Vostok. The huge craft hurtled in an orbit from 106 to 146 miles, circling the earth at 17,400 miles per hour.

Aboard Spacecraft III were two dogs, Pcholka and Mushka, as well as other animals and plant life. Superbly equipped with new instruments for transmitting vital physiologolical data back from space, the heavy ship radioed reports of its operation in space. It contained also a new automatic control system, linked to an electronic computer device being tested in space for the first time. And while the spacecraft orbited, everything worked to perfection.

After several orbits in which invaluable biological data flashed to recorders on the earth, the scientists gave the signal for Spacecraft III to descend. Once again the reaction jets flamed in space. The spaceship turned slowly until its electronic brain commanded the new attitude to be held. Another relay clicked home, a switch closed, and the powerful retro-rockets ignited with their white heat.

Spacecraft III decelerated in its orbital dash around the earth. With several hundred miles per hour of its great speed dissipated, the spaceship began to descend into the atmosphere.

But something was wrong. Almost immediately the tracking stations flashed the news; the spaceship was plunging back down toward the earth at the wrong angle of entry. The automatic stabilization system was not functioning properly, and the shield to ward off the searing heat of re-entry—heat measured in thousands of degrees—did not protect the spaceship.

That was all. Unseen by any eyes except as a sudden, blinding streak of light in the heavens, Spacecraft III yielded to the awesome temperatures of re-entry. Metal glowed red, then white with heat. The metal softened, then began to run molten. Seconds later Spacecraft III was transformed into a catastrophic meteor, disappearing into ashes that drifted slowly down toward the earth.

It was a mistake that, inevitably, had to happen. Sooner or later, in so vast and ambitious a program, an instrument would fail, an electrical system would falter, and flaming disaster would result.

Not until several weeks later were we informed of the failure. As we learned later, not until a battery of psychologists was in position to observe our every reaction, hear our every word, did we receive the news that a spacecraft of a type similar to Vostok, had shredded into a flaming mass on its re-entry. Our instructor emphasized slowly and deliberately that, had one among us been aboard that spaceship, the blazing end would have included the man, and incinerated him in a fiery death.

One man spoke for all of us. He turned to his fellow cosmonauts and grinned. "Well," he said, "that will teach them to be more careful with their equipment. Maybe they'll even make those scientists pay for the spacecraft out of their own pockets!"

We laughed loudly. We never saw the fervent handclasp of two psychologists watching us from the side of the room, the sudden sign of delight in their eyes. For they knew beyond question that at that moment their exhaustive selection over the last eighteen months was beginning to return its dividends.

6. Chamber of Horrors

"Silence . . ."

The young medical officer paused, thought for a moment, then continued his orientation to our training group; we were newly arrived at an Air Force research center.

"Silence can be a wonderful thing," the doctor continued. "It can relax nervous tension; indeed, it may even build strength into the various body muscles and systems. It calms the brain, acts in a beneficial manner to the host as well—you."

He smiled in an unpleasant manner. "That kind of silence, comrades, is what we experience at night, or when we are at rest at some vacation place. Essentially it is the only brand of silence to which you have so far been subjected.

"Here we will introduce you to silence you never knew existed. One might say that silence can be a devastating thing. It can strike you with all the force of a thunderbolt . . ."

We looked at one another, mystified.

". . . it is a silence than you will not find even in the Arctic or on the steppes." His voice suddenly became serious. "This is silence, comrades, that can literally drive you out of your mind."

He stepped down from a small stage. "Please follow me."

We walked down a long corridor and into an enormous room filled with elaborate and often mystifying research equipment and facilities. Scientists and engineers in white lab coats worked intently on many different projects, stepping over wires and cables that snaked their way in profusion throughout the room. A low but constant din came from every corner of the giant laboratory, and brilliant lights flooded the separate working areas. The doctor explained—most unsatisfactorily. "You will see and do things here that you have never seen or done before—and perhaps will never do again. That's up to each of you, mostly. But I assure you that in this place you will need every ounce of physical and mental fitness that you possess. No; let me rephrase that, comrades. I do not assure you of this—it is a *warning* for you. This is going to be tough."

It was.

One of the longest-standing research efforts of Soviet scientists has been the study of the maximum endurable stress of the human body under all possible conditions—researching and analyzing the points at which the body's organisms break down. They related their experiments to as many different aspects of human life as was possible, and they studied the widest range of occupations, from farmers to jet pilots, from bus drivers to deep-sea divers, from coal miners to Arctic explorers. They did not want to know simply when and under what conditions a body broke down—but *why*.

The key to such breakdowns lay in the body's secret of surviving unexpected or difficult conditions—adaptability. It is obvious to any doctor that the human body can absorb unbelieveable amounts of physical punishment, but this survival, we have confirmed, depends upon a given quantity of time in which the body, i.e., the body and the mental approach of the individual, can familiarize itself with its new surroundings. Any deep-sea diver worth his salt knows to a fathom the limits of his capabilities in the ocean; knowing this, familiar with the problems, he can then definitely increase the range of his capabilities. It is the same with other people in other areas of endeavor, and it has been on this basis that our doctors first attacked the problems of man in supersonic flight and all its regimes—and then struck out at the more diversified and intensive dangers that arose from flight into, through, and returning from space.

We have been fortunate in that the Academy of Sciences has in the past, as at present, afforded this series of studies the highest research priority in the country. The moment that our leaders decided that the Soviet Union was to commit itself to an all-out program of cosmic flight, our scientists were able to expand immediately into the cosmic-biological sciences from their broad base of aviation medicine. A picked team of brilliant engineers received a crash priority for a top-secret project—the maximum possible simulation of cosmic flight in the laboratory. Or, more precisely, in a network of laboratories. Having worked with—under—these men, we learned early in our relationship that they are immensely proud of their accomplishments.

When our first satellite shot into orbit, there were in the Soviet Union many large centrifuges and flight simulators built specifically for cosmic flight research. Our scientists were well aware that in both the United States and England there were barely six centrifuges that were of true practical use for pilot training. This is but one example, but it reflects the solid foundation of preparations that had been under way for so long in the biology of space flight.

For two years before our space flights we trained on simulators that even today are not identified in the United States—our only competitor in cosmic flight and exploration. It is with regret that I am unable to reveal the details of such equipment, because it is fascinating not only in its design, but in its effects upon myself and the other cosmonauts. Until conditions allow a more wholesale exchange of "hardware details," however, this matter lies entirely out of my own hands.

Beyond question, however, these simulators are the weirdest, most unnatural devices ever constructed. They have but one purpose: to get man into space as rapidly as possible commensurate with his safety. They guaranteed only one thing: that the man who could withstand their deliberately programmed terrors—and I do not use the word in error—could withstand virtually anything, and through his ordeal remain calm.

"That, comrades, is the essence of the course you will follow in your roles as cosmonauts," a scientist explained before one machine. "To keep calm no matter what transpires; everything follows from this one basic premise."

My first introduction to the nightmare tests that would decide which among us would lead the others into space was the Chamber of Silence. It might have been, in its effectiveness, something right out of the worst of medieval times. The chamber was an elaborately constructed shell, suspended on rubber shock absorbers and mounted in the center of a sprawling laboratory. The mounting and the shock absorbers guaranteed that the intent of the chamber —absolute silence—would receive no interference from even the slightest vibration of a man's footsteps along the floor of the laboratory. It had two very small glass portholes, each containing two layers of exceptionally thick glass, which could be sealed with a metal cover from the outside. One door provided entry and egress, a door more than sixteen inches thick—the thickness of the walls themselves.

Inside, the scene resembled at first glance the interior of a monk's cell; a hard steel bed, a small wooden table, a large board on the wall divided into numbered squares and, in the center of the room, an exact replica of the seat from the Vostok spaceship. During our initial tests in the room we had a television set, a television camera, and a pair of headphones. After the first few tests, these items were removed.

We crowded inside the room a few at a time. Even with the chamber door open and the sounds of the activity in the laboratory drifting in, the atmosphere within the chamber was absolutely oppressive. We examined with the greatest care every single piece of equipment, every item in the room, and we marveled at the fact that when we spoke to one another our voices were unrecognizable. Words came out flat and unreal, but unusually loud.

Then, still together in a group, we closed the chamber door. The effect was as if a prison sentence had been imposed upon us; it was absolutely uncanny. Instantly it seemed as if invisible fingers had jammed thick wads of sound-absorbent cotton into our ears. It didn't take long for the feeling to strike us that the walls seemed to be bending over, moving in; each of us wanted just to get *out*. Gagarin yanked open the door, and we stepped back into the open laboratory, where the scientists laughed at our reactions.

Once away from the chamber we became gratefully aware of even the faintest noises and, strangely, apprehensive of the time when we would return—alone—to the chamber. I say strangely because our exposure to the chamber had been so brief, and yet its impact was so great.

One by one we returned to the laboratory to enter the Chamber of Silence. Each of us found the chamber to be—well, perhaps "eerie" is a poor word, but certainly adequate enough from the viewpoint of the cosmonauts. We discussed among each other our ideas for helping to stave off the oppressive effects of the silence, but this failed to provide any real help. The Chamber of Silence was like a mirror of truth; you came face to face with yourself, and sometimes the need to rush away became virtually over-powering.

I did not like the chamber. The silence crashed against me with what seemed to be physical force. It was not a matter of my being upset or fearful of that incredible lack of sound; I just did not *like* it. My dislike became intense and on my third or fourth time in the chamber I suddenly discovered something akin to low waves of nausea moving through me. I was startled, for never in my life had I become ill in this fashion.

Each time I felt a reaction such as this one I reported to the doctors outside the chamber simply by speaking aloud; microphones in the room picked up my voice. One scientist asked if the nausea were strong; my answer was no, and that despite its discomfort it would not interfere with my work. I found that by sitting quietly in the pilot's seat and concentrating as hard as I could on some other subject I could not only ignore the stomach discomfort, but could even help in eliminating it greatly.

Again and again I returned to the chamber, with two sessions a day for several days, while the scientists observed everything I did. By the third day I felt much more at ease in the room of silence, and the nausea was only a memory. The doctors instructed me to sit on the Vostok seat, then ran me through tests of reading passages from a technical manual or a newspaper. They told me to work mathematical computations by studying the board on the wall with its numbered squares. The tests were not at all difficult, but obviously each was designed to establish a performance-level reference by the doctors. At times the monotony of the chamber tests was broken when a scientist's face appeared on the closed-circuit television screen, but these interruptions became fewer and fewer.

The repeated "flights" in the chamber had become annoying, but now they reached levels of acute psychological discomfort. Each additional visit to the chamber became greater in time. The minutes dragged on into long hours of confinement in the chamber, which became a serious problem when additional requirements fell upon me. All contact with the outside world ended. . . .

I sat in a room devoid of sound, empty of echoes, stripped of the familiar world of noises we take so much for granted that their absence strikes almost as a physical blow. The temperature was comfortable, the light adequate enough, but that was all. For all I knew, the world beyond those thick walls had vanished in a blaze of flame or by some sorcery. I was alone. I counted numbers into the thousands; I solved endless mathematical problems to myself; I read aloud and after a time even burst out into song simply to create noise. This latter move might well have been a sign of some desperation, as anyone who has listened to my voice would gladly testify.

When I satisfied the doctors and scientists that I could remain for their required time periods without any ill effects—the nausea never returned during this phase of the program—they only nodded to themselves, and announced quite without any seeming concern that I could begin the next phase of the isolation tests in the Chamber of Silence.

That was all they said; they meant much more than their words revealed. In essence, they began to tighten the screws on me. "Cosmonaut Titov, in your next test you will not talk. You will not make any sound, not a word, not an outcry. You are not even to move. You must sit in the Vostok seat. No sound, no movement. Any violation of these requirements constitutes a failure of the tests. We are ready now to begin. . . ."

To comment on this to the doctors would have been ridiculous. Without a word I turned and climbed into the chamber, settling down in the now familiar Vostok pilot seat. The heavy door swung shut and was sealed from the outside.

An avalanche of no-sound crashed into and over me, sweeping me along. And I . . . sat. I did not move. My lips remained closed; I did not cough or sneeze or mutter. I just . . . sat. I could almost visualize wave after wave of silence breaking over me, dragging me down into an impossible world of unreality. I fought back by concentrating intensely, fiercely, not to yield to the almost over-powering demand simply to cry out, to shout at the top of my lungs, to scream an invective at the silence and destroy it forever.

I did none of these things. I . . . sat, silently, unmoving. I appeared as a statue, immobilized in my seat. But within my mind there was furious activity. I dreamed elaborate pictures. I studied every minute detail, paused to look and touch and smell and listen. In my mind I heard a roaring orchestration of all the sounds that ever were.

Until, for a moment, I forgot . . . and the leaden sound crushed harder and harder.

I cursed myself, and returned to the intense concentration. It worked. When finally the door opened, I was startled at the sudden explosion of the noise. Then I grinned weakly to myself; the door opened quietly, smoothly. But I had heard no sound for so long.

When I emerged the doctors smiled happily at me. I smiled back with good reason; I had passed the roughest tests to date with flying colors. That much I deduced; the doctors never said a word about any man's performance, but it was obvious that the tougher were the tests, the better was our individual conduct.

At night we discussed with each other the tests and their different characteristics, and we learned quickly by these comparisons that we had reached a new phase in our training. The tests were not at all standard; each man was now being tested, and graded, according to his individual capabilities. Each day's meticulous reports, filled in by the doctors, scientists and the psychologists, went before a select review board—people we had never met and whose existence we knew nothing about. Not until much later did we learn of their specific and insistent surveillance of everything happening with us.

And, also later, we were provided the explanation for the differing gradients of the tests. "We do not intend to repeat any of our manned flights," a scientist said. "Each one has its own and very specific contribution to make to the total. Naturally, each successive launching and flight will be more complex, more difficult for the pilot . . . although the difficulties to be overcome certainly will be balanced by the experience accumulated by each man's predecessors. . . ."

Thus, without our knowledge, we were subject at all times to the unobtrusive classification process. Each one of us had already been provisionally assigned to a particular flight into space, and our tests and training were already being altered slightly to meet the anticipated needs of that flight.

This was something that we did not know and, obviously, we could not appreciate the external appearances and effects of these variations in the program. Without any doubt the pressure upon us would have been eased greatly had we been led to understand the nature of this classifying activity. But the rule was simple and effective: the details of the forthcoming flights were still the close secret of no more than a few scientists. Despite our position as the cosmonauts who would actively participate in those flights, there existed no *need* for us to know these details. Ergo—they did not tell us.

With some help, however, I might well have guessed that my own future assignment would be an extended flight through space. My tests in the Chamber of Silence finally became so different from the other cosmonauts that I anticipated long before the fact the multiple-orbit mission I would one day carry out. All the cosmonauts had completed their work, with each man enduring several days of continuous testing in the chamber. They resigned themselves to the unpredictable procedures of the doctors. The door closed behind them, they settled down comfortably in the chair, carried out their orders and fulfilled their tasks, knowing perfectly well that their stay could be anywhere from ten minutes to forty-eight hours. The maximum duration in the chamber for the other men was a stretch for one cosmonaut of ninety-six hours.

This man—later to be given the assignment of Cosmonaut 3— startled everyone with his completely relaxed adaptability to the chamber. Other men emerged with weary expressions on their faces, delighted to be rid finally of the oppressive lack of sound in which they had lived for days. But Cosmonaut 3 walked cheerily into the chamber carrying with him a painter's easel, canvas and palette. The doctors and his fellow cosmonauts were at first hilarious over this move, and then we were all examined. The man's adaptability was incredible.

In the utter silence of the chamber he painted in a complete and rapt absorption—and his work was beautiful! It is still prized by the doctors who have since framed and hung the beautiful renderings on their walls.

The psychologists watched through their television scanner as the man painted a scene with meticulous care. In his painting every leaf of a birch tree stood out magically, pierced by the sun's rays. The psychologists signaled impatiently for the chamber temperature to build up gradually. Steadily the warmth of the room increased . . . several hours later the cosmonaut was hard at work painting ski slopes and scenes of blizzards along the steppes. Whether he realized it or not, he was psychologically maintaining a temperature level of his body that astonished his doctors and delighted the psychologists. Later, when assigned to the chamber without his canvas and paints—and restricted to his work assignments—Cosmonaut 3 was able to apply the same intensive concentration to his work, and emerged finally with a perfect record under the stress of his tests.

I walked into the chamber for what was to be—without my knowledge at the outset—my final test. A small refrigerator in the room had been filled with sufficient food to last for several weeks, but then the refrigerator was always filled, and this provided no clue to the planned duration of the test. Minimum sanitary facilities were provided. The Vostok seat also had been modified so that the entire seat could be tilted back for sleeping. Except for the physical necessity of bowel movements, and for obtaining food, my orders were to remain in the seat.

I had work to do. The seat had been fitted with control equipment, and around me were instrument panels and controls.

Behind me the door slowly closed. Each day, as the minutes slowed more and more in their passing, I performed my duties. I spoke to the controllers outside, but only as if they were technicians on the ground, while I sat before the panel of a ship actually in flight. The instruments were real enough; they simulated precisely what would be happening if I were whirling around and around the planet. I was required to issue reports every ten minutes for hours at a time; sometimes I spoke to the scientists only once or twice a day; sometimes at two-hour intervals, right around the clock.

They never spoke to me of a subject that seemed to be forbidden

—the day of my release. This question loomed larger and larger in my mind, but to have voiced it aloud would, I believed, have broken down my resistance completely. It would be a sign of weakness, and I rebelled at the idea, forcing it back in my mind as it struggled like a live thing for its release.

The doctors and scientists were insidious in the manner in which they eased the number and frequency of tasks away from me. Without my awareness of the change, I faced longer and longer stretches of hours with nothing to do. And those tasks that I did fill were hopelessly, boringly monotonous.

Sleep was my blessing, but unless I kept to a planned schedule of sleep, I learned quickly enough that I slept fitfully, without rest, and became irritated for the few minutes in which I escaped from the chamber. We were all taught from the beginning of our training to sleep and then awake almost to the exact minute for which we had been programmed. We could go to sleep, and be assured of waking four, six or eight hours later until we ceased to marvel at our own ability to do so.

The hours dragged and dragged interminably. I had learned early in the program that the Chamber of Silence could affect a man in a manner he could not believe was possible. When you are placed in a room where the echoes vanish, where the only sound is that of your voice—flat and unreal—the silence becomes a physical entity.

Strange sounds crawl into your mind. You hear—literally hear—the sound of the blood pulsing through your ears. The sound of breathing becomes a hoarse, wheezing sound that can—to the mind weak from the onslaught of silence—become a frightening, roaring bellows. A man cannot allow this to happen to him, and I fought it desperately. When these are the sounds that intrude into the Chamber of Silence, the danger of collapse, of failure, is very real.

I sang and whistled and hummed every song I could recall. I remembered back—slowly, carefully, meticulously—through every incident my mind would yield. I studied the instruments of every airplane I ever flew, made minute inspections of its equipment, reviewed the technical manuals and the textbooks. In my mind I laboriously took apart an entire automobile. Very neatly I laid out on the ground each piece of equipment; every spring, nut, bolt, washer, screw, gear—everything. Slowly I rebuilt that car, assembled the motor, started it, tested it, checked and altered and inspected it. Then it vanished from my mind, its last possible element having been dissected until I feared for the repetition of the event, and my inability to maintain some semblance of the accurate passing of time.

For a while I listened carefully to the beating of my heart, noting the spacing and interval of each thudding sound within my chest, and counting the beats—a human metronome within me, clattering away as it pulsated. That in itself became a warning; so engrossed had I become in the monotonous sound of the beats that it was with an abrupt warning of fear that I realized I was hearing each beat of my heart with a crash. The sound in my mind had grown in volume to such proportion that all reality seemed to flee. Angrily I cursed myself for this lapse, and avoided with a vengeance the pitfall of total absorption in a constant, hypnotic repetition.

The door opened on the fifteenth day. My feelings at the sight of that suddenly yawning space, at the anxious eyes peering in, are beyond all description. . . .

For several days afterward I enjoyed the blessed tumult of classrooms. Every clunk, bang, whimper, scratch, gasp, wheeze, knock, clang and screech came to my ears as music, and never could I have believed that the ordinary classroom sounds that attended our technical lectures could have been so filled with what I regarded as the wonderful melody of the everyday world!

Then, back to the physical training—the adaptation process, as we had come to label the ingenious schedule of our doctors and scientists. Nothing could ever approach specifically the nature of

the Chamber of Silence, but this was no guarantee that our beneficial tormenters could not produce other devices equally grim in
their own light—and startling to contemplate.

We looked upon the centrifuge almost as an old friend. Being
whirled around until centrifugal forces mashed us down into our
seats as though we were buried beneath tons of stone was almost
a pleasure compared to those infinite number of minutes suffered
in the Chamber of Silence. But I had failed to anticipate the different needs of cosmic flight, as opposed to my experience in the
centrifuge with jet flight in mind. Again and again I was flung
around a giant control room at the end of a long steel arm, the
increasing speed simulating the continuing acceleration of a rocket,
and squeezing me with all the effect of an enormous invisible hand
that gripped me helplessly in its steel fingers.

It is a sensation well known to most pilots who have traveled the
path of the centrifuge, but to us, the effects were far more severe.
We would encounter forces in acceleration, and then in the
deceleration of our return to the atmosphere, that could render us
helpless within our spacecraft. Tolerance to these savage gravity
forces resulted from many factors—mental approach, physical
well-being, devices to aid the body in its pressure and shifting of
the body fluids, the direction in which our bodies received the
forces and—it was unpleasant to realize—from the experience of
continued exposure. We withstood without any great difficulty the
worst we received, and each night after a period on the centrifuge
sleep came quickly—after having our limbs turn to lead, our blood
to mercury, our eyeballs to blazing points—ad nauseum.

Assuming a man has behind him proper and extensive training
and experience, a cosmonaut under ideal conditions may take in
his stride a sustained force of seven to eight times that of normal
gravity without damage to his internal organs. The gravity forces
must be applied in a direction from the chest through the body
toward the back for the greatest physical resistance of the body.

Wearing a pressure suit, a set of artificial bladders around the stomach, thighs and legs, lying comfortably on a seat molded to the contours of the body—a man can take even greater pressure.

Our requirements were brutal. Each of us was considered successful in the program only after we sustained the bruising force of fifteen times the force of gravity for a period of several minutes. For brief seconds a man could withstand much higher forces.

No man enjoyed more respect and admiration from the cosmonauts—as well as our doctors, who gave us detailed medical reports of his tests—than an American. This was an Air Force medical officer, Colonel John Stapp, who proved his theories by what he considered his infallible method—subjecting himself to the worst that might happen. We listened spellbound as a doctor explained to us the peak of Stapp's career—his ride aboard a sled propelled by rockets that reached a speed of 632 miles per hour. But his manner of ending the test was unbelievable. The American doctor had crashed deliberately into a water barrier, and from his awesome speed slammed to a dead stop in only 1.4 seconds. Our instructor told us his deceleration force—more than forty times the force of gravity! We were stunned at this figure—to say nothing of the confidence we gained from its lack of permanent ill effects upon the doctor-scientist who made the test.

But even that kind of a ride would have been preferable to the Iron Maiden in which I spent several hours. Technicians taped medical sensors to my body to record the functions of my nervous system, then clothed me in the complete space suit to be worn aboard the Vostok. I climbed into a small, padded metal box, which bore an unhappy resemblance to a coffin, just large enough to hold a man and a replica of the Vostok pilot seat. The technicians strapped me down, adjusted the height of the arm, head and foot-rests, and checked all the electrical connections. With impassive faces they closed the lid of the box.

I found myself in absolute, total darkness. I could not move. All about me the soft, shaped padding pressed down like some horrible, glutinous mass. Then began a torture that would have been hailed as sheer genius by the Inquisitors.

A voice crackled in my ears through the headphones. "All right, Titov; we begin now." That was all; then I sensed movement. I couldn't *see* anything—I judged movement by a changing pressure on my body.

From a control panel in the corner of the laboratory, a doctor began the test. Slowly the coffin began to revolve on a spindle, turning over and over in an incessant motion. The doctor worked a second switch, and another movement began. The two giant metal arms gripping the spindle began to move about in a huge circle. Inside the coffin, I was spinning over and over while the arms carried me up towards the roof of the laboratory, and then down and around again in a huge arc before starting up once more. Inside the coffin I partially sensed the movements, and noted distinctly in the coal-blackness of the coffin that the movements were being increased steadily in their speed.

Then—unknown to me, of course—the doctor moved a third control switch, and in a pleasantly macabre fashion, he introduced a third plane of motion. This sent the already spinning, tumbling coffin into another circular direction so that now I was being whirled about in three different directions—all at the same time! It was not a test created essentially for its diabolic motions—the spaceship in orbit could easily be whirled out of control by uneven forces, and sent into a violent tumbling motion about three axes, just as I was experiencing at this moment. Throughout the entire test the doctors required me to maintain a continuing conversation reporting the sensations I experienced, and how I felt.

How does a man describe the impossible? Except for our own cosmonauts and the astronauts of the United States, no man has ever been subjected to such unnatural, *unearthly* pressures and simultaneous application of these pressures. One thing I could say, and with conviction—a feeling of nausea and body sickness that persisted for several hours afterward, then abated. Gradually, however, I became accustomed to the sensation of the three-axis motion, and came to understand why the doctors were so convinced that I would cease to be bothered with the feelings of nausea.

The tests continued, and once again I found myself on our original transportation to the cosmos—a refinement of the vibrating bus we endured during our original selection program. But the experience of being rattled about gently at two hundred times a minute was almost relaxing. The vibration frequency was slightly higher than that of a barber's vibro-massage, but gave me no trouble just so long as I remembered to relax, instead of tensing my body. Then it seemed as if my teeth were about to fall out.

Taking turns with the other cosmonauts, I perspired freely and alternately felt as if I were freezing to death in a thermal chamber. Wearing my complete space suit, I was lowered slowly into a deep water tank until I was several feet below the surface of the water. It was an effective way of testing the suit and its breathing apparatus. . . .

Nothing commanded our attention so much as our discussions on the one sensation of cosmic flight which we could not reproduce on the ground—the weightlessness of sustained zero-gravity during orbital flight. And even in modified aircraft—fighters and transports—we could gain some insight of weightlessness only for the briefest periods of time. By having the pilot fly the airplane through a precise parabolic curve through the sky—a careful soaring "up and over" through a long curve—we were weightless for time periods up to about one minute. In padded transport cabins we floated and spun, drifted gently or whirled about, squeezed food and water into our mouths, and manipulated different controls that we would have in Vostok.

I felt an unusual sense of lightness through the zero-G periods, but it was really a most pleasant sensation. My attempts to carry out different movements and to test my coordination at first presented a slight problem when consistently I showed a tendency to overreach when trying to grasp objects. Several minutes' experience under weightlessness in the airplanes apparently eliminated this problem, and for a while I simply let myself go to enjoy the sensations of zero-G. After a while I enjoyed it so much I wanted to sing!

Our biologists were not quite so entranced with the subject. Experiments with dogs in our satellites led to the conclusion that with our training and adaptability, we would have little or no difficulty in meeting the rigors of several hours of weightlessness. But they *were* concerned. . . .

Since no man had ever been weightless for more than a minute, even the most careful speculation could remain little more than an unproved treatise on the subject. Of the greatest concern to the doctors were the psychological disturbances that might arise from orbital flight. Sustained zero-G, the remoteness of the flight, concentration upon the instruments—a combination of these factors might possibly induce a state of hypnosis on a truly extended space flight.

No one knew, and we were extremely anxious to discover the solutions to these vexing problems. Finally, the doctors made their decision. There were too many unknowns involved to indulge in a brash commitment to the first manned flight. We would go slowly, and we would move carefully.

Our original plans, we learned at a special meeting, had been for a flight of several orbits—possibly as many as six, which would bring the Vostok over the approach to the prescribed landing area. But no longer. The questions looming in the minds of the doctors were too many and too extensive to risk this gamble.

The first manned orbital flight would be restricted to one orbit of the earth.

Now we knew the mission to be flown. We looked at one another and wondered who among us would be the first man ever to travel through the cosmos.

7. The Chief Constructor

If I have any regrets in respect to my training program, and later my operational flight as a cosmonaut, it is the lack of public attention given to the single most important man in the Soviet Union's cosmic flight program. His name must still remain hidden from the world until our government decides that the time is right for him to be identified, but I for one regret personally (as do all the others who have worked for and with this outstanding person) his long anonymity. He is a man who walks with the giants who have affected and even made history, and he can be known as yet only by his title—the Chief Constructor.

This is his official name, and its unfortunate ring of something out of H. G. Wells obscures the enormous respect in which he is held by his fellow scientists and certainly by the cosmonauts. He is the man responsible for Vostok, for its design, its innovations, its construction and testing. He is the one man more than anyone else who knows so deeply what is happening in space with his beloved handiwork. He knows every line, every pound, every piece of metal and glass in his creation, and he has left no effort undone to transfer this intimacy with his cosmic machine to each of us who might travel within its interior through a vastness beyond the world of men.

Vostok is essentially and primarily his own creation. True, a scientific staff assists his work, as they have done in the past. But

113

unlike many large aircraft projects where the winged machine emerges as the result of many minds and many hands, Vostok springs in the main from the mind of this one individual. Small wonder, then, that without the slightest attempt on his part to do so, he commands the highest respect of his nation—technical, academic, and scientific.

This much I can say of him: he is one of the most influential— and highly decorated—men in the Soviet Academy of Sciences. Throughout all of Russia's scientific and government circles he stands undisputed as the father of our space program. He has from the beginning proved the kind of a catalyst with which an entire nation may be spurred on to great deeds against great odds. We are fortunate to have not only his scientific and engineering genius, but also his hammering drive against all obstacles.

Like his close personal friend, Keldysh, Chairman of the Academy, the Chief Constructor throughout his life has specialized in engineering and metallurgy, particularly as they are applied to the dual sciences of aerodynamics and hydrodynamics. His specialty ranges from the liquid surface of the earth to far beyond its atmosphere; with a colleague he designed the famed hydrofoil ships, those amazing riverboats that carry three hundred passengers at speeds up to one hundred miles per hour on the larger rivers of the country.

His road toward the stars has not been without its thorns. Like Academecian Keldysh he was more than once in dire straits with the Stalinists for his passionate and insistent belief that the Soviet Union must waste no time in beginning a vast program for cosmic flight. And as happened with the farsighted in many lands around the world, he faced storms of derision and opposition from his scientific colleagues for such fanciful proposals. But has it not ever been this way? Our training as cosmonauts required us to understand the paths that led to the first open doors to space, and the similarity in these problems of men like the Chief Constructor are amazingly strong. More than once we heard from our instructors of the tremendous advantages that the United States threw away by denying the genius and the foresight of their Dr. Goddard, who in our own country holds his place of honor as the first man in the world to fire a liquid-propellant rocket. What position would our contemporaries hold today had they pursued vigorously this position of once leading the way?

We enjoyed the good fortune once to be with the Chief Constructor as he spoke freely on the future; it was an occasion not included in our technical and training curriculum. I believe the man was simply in one of his rarer expansive moods, and with the gleaming sides of our training equipment providing a background fitting to the conversation, he told not of his dreams, but more realistically of his plans, for the near future.

"You represent only the smallest of the small first steps of man," he said, not unkindly, "but without such a first step we could go nowhere, do nothing; we would have to accept the sentence of eternal imprisonment on this world. And man is destined for better things than to live out his life on this small sphere with its closed cycle of life. The stars do not shine in the heavens for effect; they are a call, a beckoning . . . .

"After your first ascents into that void beyond us, we will know how to adapt, how to utilize our new energies and talents. Tomorrow's Sputniks will be practicable devices instead of research instruments with which to glean the secrets of new energies, of space itself. We will build satellites by which to navigate the ships and the planes bound closely to the surface of this earth; we will communicate by our orbiting laboratories; we will study the earth and our moon, the planets, and the farthest reaches of the cosmos. And when a hundred years are behind us, we will still be taking our first step in respect to galactic time and galactic distances.

"But we will do it. It will not be many years hence before you personally will tread the surface of the moon, before you will build the first crude shelters for yourselves and your comrades who will be waiting impatiently to join you on the second world of man.

We will do it; of that I am certain! Perhaps for you this is a newly-discovered dream of tomorrow, but comrades, I tell you it is the same dream I knew before you were born. The words, the dream . . . no, they have not changed. It is just that everything is now that much closer than before. And you are the men who will make it come true for me . . . for all of us."

But all this came later, much later after we first met this remarkable man. At the time of our first meeting, the entire group of cosmonauts were near the end of their training that included theoretical studies. We drove to a secluded cluster of buildings, identified as a special institute of rocketry. Here, to greet us, the Chief Constructor decided personally to give us our first lecture.

The man was much younger than I had anticipated; by virtue of his reputation and his many years in the field, I expected to find an elderly, bearded scientist in the last few years of his life. Such was not the case. He dressed simply, and his clothes revealed a powerful physical build. I found it impossible to guess his age, for his hair was touched only lightly with gray. His eyes sparkled with life, and his massive shoulders and arms could have come from a steel foundry, for all we knew. Above all, he certainly was anything but the tired old scientist puttering about in a laboratory!

When he spoke, his voice commanded our every moment of attention. He spoke with a frankness and honesty that gripped our imagination, for he interspersed his candor with a constant vision of the future in which he believed so deeply. It was not possible to listen to this man and avoid being swept along by the strength of his beliefs. He outlined for us the progress of his scientific and engineering staff in fuels, metallurgy, propulsion, and electronics since he and his men cheered the success of their first space firing with Sputnik I. He emphasized the lessons we had learned with each successive firing.

The sound of a pin dropping in the room could have been heard as he explained to us the schedule for the flights of the first three cosmonauts to go into space—and then he dropped a small bombshell by revealing that the three men had long ago been selected. Not until the scientists and the doctors decided that the time was appropriate, he explained, would those three men be informed of their identity.

I was, frankly, deeply moved by this man's fantastic depths of knowledge and the grasp of a subject that only several years before enjoyed the scorn more than the respect of most of the world's scientific body. We gained more of a feeling for what we were doing, and why, from this initial encounter than from any other single event of our entire training program.

For the several days following, we studied the details of the enormous rockets with which our scientists were making their unprecedented advances in space. It was not enough to be impressed with the size and power of these giant carrier vehicles, or to sit in awe as we watched thousands of feet of film of their tests and launchings. As the men who would actually ride these blazing volcanoes of energy upward from the earth, we had to add to our growing accumulation of knowledge the precise machinery of their operation, and exactly how their performance would relate to the flights we ourselves would make.

At the institute we received our first detailed reports of an area that none of us had yet seen, but which we would come to know in great detail. This was Baikonur, the magic name of Soviet space rocketry, our last stone on the earth before stepping deeply into the cosmos. Baikonur was a city, but not really so. It had been created out of the need for a port from which men could sail in their fiery vessels into space, and Baikonur looked its part. It flashed with lights of all colors and description, lights that burned day and night, in storm and clear weather, lights that gleamed from lofty towers or outlined the shape of monstrous steel platforms, lights that drifted along the roads or shone from the helicopters and the airplanes that seemed to drift incessantly around and above the city of space.

Baikonur is a sprawling, electronic, technological womb for the fires we intended to blaze in the vacuum high over us. Massive steel and concrete buildings dotted its landscape, huddled beneath the looming gantries and workstands. Rounded concrete humps in the earth revealed the position of the thick blockhouses, where select groups of men attended the final electronic orchestration that led to the crashing finale of ignition and the ascent of the giants from their steel clamps anl launch rings. And deep beneath this once-secret city, workmen long ago carved out an enormous space. Here they built a giant underground command and control center, the core of all our space operations, the network from where all our activities were controlled and commanded.

Throughout the great launching site, surrounded by tall birch and fir trees that rolled with gentle hills, cars and trucks moved almost constantly. A four-lane concrete super-highway cut through the launch center itself, rolled away from the last row of gates, and disappeared in the distance toward Moscow. Other roads, beyond the perimeter of Baikonur, led to giant housing developments where the many thousands of workmen and scientific personnel lived.

Baikonur is one of the most recent—and certainly the largest— of all our launching sites for space operations. Among the reasons for its selection was its remoteness, plus the vital fact that Baikonur's position places the launch site at the apex of a triangular firing range that stretches all the way into Siberia and the Arctic. It enjoys comparatively mild weather, and its elevation of fifteen hundred feet lies on the same latitude as Paris. An additional factor in the selection of Baikonur was the convenient proximity to a number of major research centers and industrial rocket plants.

The Air Force maintains a severe administrative control over Baikonur's operations, assisted by a joint senior staff of civil engineers, employees from the Academy of Sciences, and Air Force officers. The Baikonur commander is responsible directly to the Space Commission in Moscow, and is free from any outside interference in his operations, except for those times when the Chief

Constructor and his immediate colleagues are physically present at Baikonur to assume direct control over all activities during a launch into space. At these moments Baikonur assumes a vitality that is impossible to capture with words; it is a feeling, a sense of urgency that keeps lights burning day and night in the offices as well as on the looming workstands.

Included in our detailed interrogations of all that occurs at Baikonur were descriptions of its logistical support, its manpower, and, above all, a study of the paper river that flows every day into the launching center. At Baikonur engineers study carefully the processed results of rocket firings at other ranges of the Soviet Union, and no one distant event created so great a distrubance as the reports of the sensational test firings late in 1961 (I was to note much later after my first visits to Baikonur) of new booster rockets—the rockets that would carry ponderous weights carefully and precisely to the moon.

But while Baikonur commanded the center of the spotlight in the business end of our space activities, the critical brain center for all our work went on without interruption in another building several hundred miles distant. At this secret location great electronic calculators outnumber the human force by more than ten to one—for here is the coordinating-computer control room. This center and Baikonur are linked invisibly by literally thousands of miles of telephone lines, radio cables and closed-circuit television, and it is a flat joke among the staff of each center that they cannot even light a cigarette in one place without the move being observed by a dozen men watching television screens in the other center. For all their separation of miles, they are in the electronic sense under the same roof.

We came finally to understand the essential performance of every element of both Baikonur and the computer center, for from these two places would come the decisions and the commands that might well dictate our safety in space—or our fiery end as the result of a failure or a miscalculation. The more we knew of the operation of these centers, the better we could integrate in our own minds the superb interweaving of computer capability with human decision as it would affect us.

At our final training meeting at Baikonur, attended by the Chief Constructor, we were asked to remain in the lecture room as our instructors left. The scientist walked past each one of us, handing out a small, five-sided piece of metal.

"This is an exact replica of the emblems our second lunar rocket carried to the surface of the moon. Perhaps one day you may bring back to me one of the originals."

He meant every word he said to us.

8. Vostok

Our visit to Baikonur prompted the next phase of training. With growing excitement we studied diagrams of our spaceship, pored over detailed drawings of its equipment and controls, its construction, propulsion systems, life support and the many thousands of items that must be crammed into the vessel to contain and support a man's life in vacuum. A feeling of new vitality swept through not only the cosmonauts, but the entire training and engineering staffs as well. As planned by the Space Commission in Moscow, our concentration upon the actual spacecraft represented the high-water mark in our long-range program aimed toward actual manned orbital flight around the planet. By now the theoretical training was a thing of the past; every step we took from this moment on pushed toward the application of our training and knowledge—application represented by one among us in space as quickly as was possible within the limitations of safety and scientific knowledge.

We still did not know the identity of the man who would make that awesome first step into the gulf that separates the different worlds of space. It mattered only in a personal vein, for there was no question that of our number, any one of the twelve cosmonauts met every requirement—and more—for that initial ascent.

And then came that morning for which we had waited so impatiently. We drove to an Air Force engineering center, guarded heavily and isolated from outside views. Guards inspected our passes and led us through a labyrinth of buildings to an enormous industrial hanger almost unbelievable in its size. We stepped through a wide door; far across the sprawling hanger floor, surrounded by a swarm of men and machines, awaited the spaceship. We walked with growing anticipation across the hanger, moving around clusters of workmen and machines. Around us the hanger echoed with the ringing sounds of generators, power drills, cranes, and heavy presses; it was a marvelous symphony of the age of space.

We stood before our spaceship. For long moments not one of us uttered a word as we stared at the beautiful lines of the spacecraft. Before us loomed a gleaming silver cylinder longer than twenty feet; under the brilliant arc lights the conical nose sparkled and flashed. She was beautiful, overwhelmingly so. Every one of us read in our minds the same thoughts, the same impressions of this wonderful vessel rushing through space with a velocity of five miles *every single second*. It was an inspiring moment, shared deeply, without need for words.

A metal stairway led to small doors in the side of the spaceship; I was on my way even as the Chief Constructor laughed and called out: "Go on . . . she's all yours. After all, you're the ones who will have to take her up."

I brushed my hands along the sleek metal skin, still marveling at the sight of the Vostok. As the other cosmonauts clambered up the stairs behind me, I squeezed through the door. The brilliant interior lighting flashed off the instruments and controls.

For several moments I stared, turning my head slowly, convincing myself that this truly was the spaceship we had waited so long to see. Vostok was much larger than I anticipated, based on my experiences in jet fighters, and quite unlike the interior of my old familiar MIG fighters. Compared to the jet the instrument panels and controls were astonishing in their simplicity.

Slowly I eased my body into the seat, settling down in the position I had found comfortable during the long months of training, especially in the Chamber of Silence. I shifted position several times, then, leaning back and relaxing, I reached out for the controls to judge their accessibility. One control seemed difficult to reach, awkward to use. Quickly I drew a pad and pencil from my tunic and made some quick sketches.

The seat dominated the entire cabin, built into a strange form of shell. I studied the seat controls and levers, checking to see the manner in which the explosive charges blew away the side of the spaceship and hurled the seat and its occupant far clear of the craft. I could not help smiling as I wondered what sort of emergency in space might be helped by an ejection seat . . .

The seat itself was extremely comfortable, but it was much too large for me; then I realized that with my space suit and other equipment, I would actually fit perfectly into its space. The suits that we wore for training were unsuitable for actual space flight; bulky and fitted out with different types of equipment, they were actually training devices. But we had already seen our attire for our voyages in the cosmos—pale blue, amazingly lightweight and strong, woven throughout with electrical leads and equipment. More familiar to me because of my experience with partial-pressure suits in the supersonic MIGs was the inner suit layer of skin-tight cotton that could be laced to fit every contour of the body; and the outer layers of rubberized capron (nylon) with their capstan pressure hoses.

I could not tear my eyes away from the spaceship's interior. I tried to drink in every detail, marveling at the miracle in which I was encased. A ship to reach out to the stars! I could not lose the feeling of awe and wonder. I relaxed, trying to imagine myself in flight. There, before me, the control panel no more than a fingertip's length away; the switches above—just right. The dials were . . . no, they were not good. I squinted, trying to see better; they were just readable, in need of improvement. Perhaps back-illumination or self-illumination. I jotted down some more notes on my pad.

Then the control handle. Slowly, carefully, I closed my hand around the handle, clinching the cold black plastic in my fist. Gently I squeezed my fingers, almost caressing the device with which I would one day control this same type of machine far beyond the earth.

An impatient bellow aroused me from my thoughts. It was Gagarin, angry, calling for me to leave so that he also could climb into the ship he waited to take away from the earth. I laughed at him and climbed out of the Vostok as he brushed his way past me, seeing only the brilliant interior of the spacecraft.

The days following were filled with a rising excitement now that we worked with the actual machine for our long-anticipated flights. To outsiders, Vostok was no more than just a machine. To us, she assumed a personality. She had her virtues and her vices, and we were anxious to be completely knowledgeable of both.

My natural curiosity of mechanical and engineering subjects caused me many sleepless nights as I lived with Vostok and the elaborate diagrams of her equipment. I went over every inch of the portholes and the snap-action manholes, studied the reaction jet system, the liquid-fueled retro-rocket module, the instruments and the controls, the equipment that kept the air fresh and constantly circulating. I practiced with the radio, television and telegraph equipment simply that I might know every square inch of the surface of this equipment; not until I could run my fingers over the communications and other equipment—with my eyes closed, in the manner of the blind—and know exactly what I touched, and what was nearby, did I consider myself even basically acquainted with that beautiful machine.

Not until then could I voice, even to myself, the ideas strong in my mind. I was enchanted with the spaceship, but not overcome by its wonder, and certainly I still possessed the means to study Vostok in a wholly objective manner. During my first meeting with the spaceship I discovered what I felt were flaws in the control setup; the instruments required improved illumination, and one particular control was awkward in its design and in its placement.

Mine were not the only objective and at times critical comments on certain aspects of Vostok's interior; yet this was natural, since we looked upon the spaceship's controls and certain other features from the hard viewpoint of the experienced pilot. And no matter how brilliant he is, or how many years he has pursued his vocation, there does not live an engineer or scientist in the world who can anticipate *all* the requirements that different viewpoints—and then experience—will dictate.

I noticed that my fellow cosmonauts felt also that there was room not so much for improvement, but for modification of certain equipment, in Vostok. At the same time they hesitated to voice their opinions to the scientists for fear they might be held up to ridicule, or even criticized for interfering in an era of engineering for which they might not properly be equipped. Past experience had more than once dictated to me the wisdom of acting in a prudent manner, but so vital a subject as Vostok—and the mission that it would carry out—commanded more than silence.

At a morning conference I laid down my sketches before the Chief Constructor. Puzzled, he looked up at me, then back to the sketches. "Sir," I said, "these are several ideas which occurred to me after spending much time with Vostok. I have put much thought into them, and they represent the view of the pilot. I hope that there may be some use in them . . ." The sentence trailed off as the scientist picked up the papers, rustling them in his hands. For several long minutes he pored over the sketches, turning from one to the other, reading my penciled notes and comparing them with the drawings.

Then: "Humph."

That was all for a while; just a very unscientific, deep-in-thought grunt. I stared at the floor and the walls and tried not to shift my weight from one foot to the other. Abruptly the Chief Constructor walked away toward his office; he stopped and turned toward me. "Well, what are you waiting for, Titov? Come along man, come along!" I hurried after him.

Another ten minutes went by in his office as he studied the

sketches anew. Then, leaning back in his chair and tapping the papers with a pencil, he looked directly at me. "You realize, Titov," he said, "that if I were to follow your recommendations it would mean just about rebuilding the entire spaceship?" His face showed not a trace of emotion.

Startled, I tried to reply, but he cut me short with a casual wave of his hand. "No, no . . . really, it's perfectly all right," he laughed. "Don't be concerned, Titov—I recall that I *did* ask for questions and suggestions. But I never expected anything like this!"

He glanced down at the papers and back to me again. "I cannot say anything about the merit of your suggestions now; I must have time in which they can be studied carefully. But I will say this much—they reflect good engineering thinking. Now, back to your duties . . ." And with that I was dismissed.

I returned to the hanger floor, elated, and quickly told my comrades what had happened. They were surprised, and apprehensive for me, at my breach of protocol. Then one by one they laughed; now that the ice was broken, they had plenty of their own ideas to recommend. Within three days time the Chief Constructor's desk overflowed with blueprints, sketches, plans, drawings, and list after list of recommendations that altered everything from the size of the pilot's entire cabin to the colors of the interior material.

That last choice item proved the straw to break the camel's back, and orderlies hastened to inform us that a special engineering meeting had been called—at once—in the office of the Chief Constructor. Harassed, half-obscured by the stacks of papers and blueprints on his desk, he addressed us in what was patently not one of his better moods.

"Gentlemen, I am astonished at your prodigious output," he began, "for I was unaware that we had in our midst so many talented and experienced engineers." We winced visibly, bringing an unexpected burst of laughter from the engineer. "You all look like children who have been caught stealing cookies. All right, all of you, come here around my desk . . . . Let me explain some of the facts of engineering life to you."

That afternoon proved to be one of the finest of our entire training program. Behind his closed doors, the Chief Constructor packed into several hours for us the cream of his engineering experience and talent. He waded neatly through mystifying principles and many different subjects (of which we knew little) that affected final decisions in the construction of the spaceship.

One by one, he dissected our ideas and proposals—and in every instance explained carefully exactly why, although they appeared sound at first glance, they were weakened by the hard facts of engineering for space flight. I was delighted at the end of the conference when I realized that several of my own proposals were *not* included in his exhaustive criticism. Several days later my hopes were confirmed when an orderly summoned me to the Chief Constructor's office.

The engineer greeted me with a roar of delight; he left his desk, grasped my arm in a powerful squeeze and half-led, half-dragged me through the hanger where the spaceship awaited us. But even from a distance sensed that something was different; the technicians no longer swarmed around the machine, but stood back in little groups. Vostok's birth—at least here on this world—was complete. The spaceship was ready for flight.

The Chief Constructor stopped so suddenly by the machine that I almost stumbled over him. He waved an arm proudly. "There she is, Titov—ready and waiting. She is finished," he cried. "Now, tell me, do you notice anything different about our space vessel?"

I looked at him, receiving only an impassive stare for an answer. I walked around Vostok, but her gleaming lines were the same as before. No, the spaceship appeared no different at all.

I climbed the stairway and peered through the hatch. They *had* made changes! Quickly I clambered into the cabin and eased into the pilot's seat, the Chief Constructor, behind me, sliding his bulk alongside me. He said nothing, but nodded for me to study the cabin carefully.

There . . . the instrument panel. Dials had been moved, gauges were clearer to read. I flicked a switch and the gauges came to life, numbers and dials standing out brilliantly but without glare. Wonderful! Instinctively I reached out toward the control that previously defied ease of operation; before my arm traveled its limit my fingers closed on the handle. That *was* good. I closed my eyes, moving my hands swiftly but carefully along the instruments and control devices I had come to know so well. Some of them were altered in their shape; others had been moved. The improvements were tremendous—and there was yet another change, for which I had no credit, but that delighted us all. The contour seat (it might also be considered a couch) was now mounted on special bearings so that in space it could actually turn in a complete circle. This would allow the cosmonaut-pilot always to be horizontal across the line of travel if he so desired. The pilot could maintain a horizontal attitude, sitting up or reclining, always in reference to the earth's horizon. Our scientists and doctors obviously deemed this system the most efficient and rewarding for flight in the weightless condition, and we never found cause to argue with this point.

Vostok was a double-compartmented spaceship with the pilot's seat mounted in the smaller compartment. In the larger space would go special test instruments and equipment, animals, cameras and other devices for extensive tests in space—all of them able to function independently of the cosmonaut's own control.

I spent several minutes looking around the cabin, observing, noting. Everything was now perfect. I looked around at our Chief Constructor, then dropped my gaze. "Thank you," I said quietly. "This is very wonderful. I assure you it will mean much to the men who ride this machine through space."

The engineer squeezed my shoulder. "Your points were well taken," he explained. "That must be obvious to you, for here they are before your eyes. Now—"he rubbed his hands briskly—"more has been done than shows on the surface . . ." And for the next half hour we remained in the spaceship, talking over the modifications to Vostok and what we might expect in the future, depending upon our experience and lessons from the first flight. The Chief

Gherman's aunt, father and mother at home

The main street at Polkovnikovo, Titov's home

Tamara greets Gherman
at Moscow's airport

Tamara

Titov as a young
Air Force officer

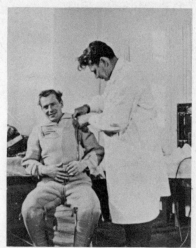

Just before take-off

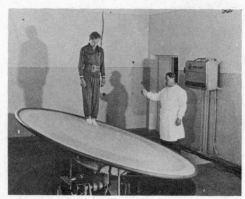

Titov on balancing table

In training

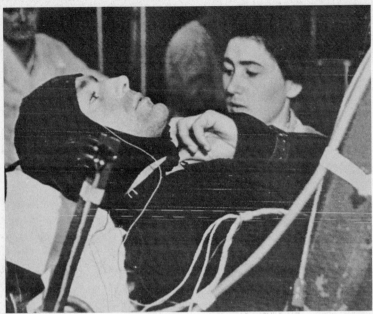

In centrifuge during training

The pilot's seat included everything
needed for survival in an emergency

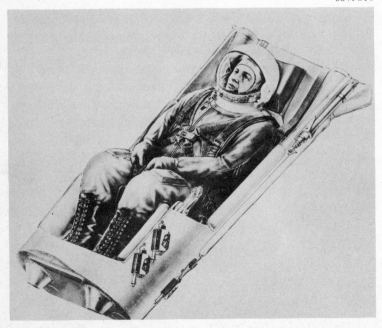

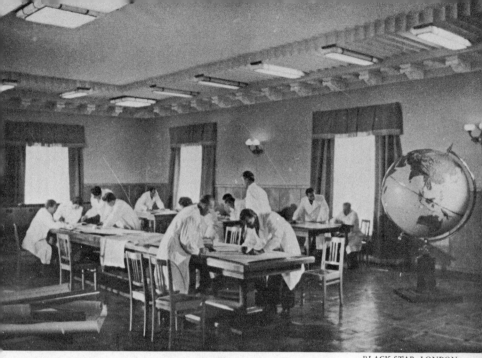

The plotting room at Baikonur

Part of the Baikonur operations room

Khrushchev, Titov and Gagarin
during Gherman's welcoming parade

Titov reports his flight
successful to Khrushchev

Purdy and Burchett
interview Titov

Gagarin and Titov

Titov in astronaut's suit

Constructor appeared delighted with the changes, for from that moment on the cosmonauts were encouraged to submit their recommendations for changes. Thus supplied with an incentive, of their own accord they spent hour after hour into the night studying the engineering details of the spaceship and, in the long run, made many invaluable contributions to improve the quality of our equipment.

But two weeks were to pass before I discovered to what extent I had struck home with my own recommendations, each of them carefully worked out in notes and blueprint-sketches. I received a special message directly from the Space Commission in Moscow, which brought resounding congratulations from the rest of our team.

I had been appointed on an equal level with the engineers to the scientific and technical council for Project Vostok! The news overwhelmed me, but of course did not detract from the tremendous advantages it gave our group of cosmonauts.

My presence after receiving this letter was mandatory at the meetings of the Project's department heads, where protocol went out the window and some healthy table-thumping served to emphasize a particular point. In all these meetings I felt delightfully comfortable and did my best to contribute worthwhile suggestions and ideas; at the same time the other cosmonauts funneled their own ideas through me to the meetings, allowing us to save time in our proposals, and permitting a pooling of talent. My studies as a cosmonaut assumed a new and far deeper meaning than before, and I waxed enthusiastic as the engineering staff went out of their way to afford me true understanding of the complex matters involved.

At one meeting a discussion so startled me with its implications of a new engineering concept that I forgot myself, and dashed out of the room to my own office—leaving behind me a room filled with astonished engineers. All that afternoon and through the night, without sleep, I struggled to commit to paper what hung in such tantalizing fashion in my mind. The next morning, unkempt and disheveled, I almost hammered down the door to the office of the Chief Constructor. In my excitement I tried to speak too quickly, stammering out words rather than presenting them in an intelligent fashion.

He pushed me firmly into a chair, forbade me to speak, and spread my sketches on his desk. His own excitement grew visibly by the moment. Nothing would please me more than to detail the contents of those papers; unfortunately, this cannot be done at this time.

No man in all the Soviet knew a greater pride than mine many months after this particular morning when, with the Chief Constructor present, my government awarded me the Order of Lenin.*

While my engineering work went on, I knew not a moment's relaxation in the grueling pace of our training schedules. Adding to this was the relentless mental pressure of advanced studies, and I began to wilt under these combined burdens.

As the weeks passed, however, I felt crushed from a problem of entirely another matter. Each day that I worked part of me rejoiced in what we were doing, but this emotion clashed with a feeling of cold dread that gripped my heart with bitter pain.

I was convinced that my emotions were not known to the others. Unknown to me, the sleepless nights I spent at home were combining with my exhausting work schedule, and finally the doctors became alarmed at my white face and worried eyes. I failed to realize that I had withdrawn from the close comradeship I shared with the other cosmonauts; nor did I sense that no longer did I visit freely with the Chief Constructor or his colleagues.

They, however, noticed what I failed to observe in myself. I could be found in a classroom or laboratory, staring at a wall or

* One of the highest decorations that the Soviet Union may award to one of its citizens, representing a contribution to Soviet progress of the greatest importance. MC.

out a window, but seeing nothing. I felt that a part of me was dying, even as we worked to breathe life into a new and wonderful adventure for all of us.

For at home, Tamara and I lived with the cruelest of personal tragedies. We had waited long and anxiously for our first child, and the rejoicing in both families knew no bounds when my son Igor joined us in life. But after several months of delighting in our child, our laughter turned to concern, and the concern to fear. Even that emotion was denied us as Igor languished, lying for hours in Tamara's arms, listless and ill. Fear would have been preferable to the cold dread that struck at our hearts.

My son Igor was dying. We could not avoid the stark and terrible truth.

Each day, as I worked and studied and trained, I could not escape the picture of Tamara in our home, fighting back her tears as she clasped our son to her—while he slowly gave up his precious life. The project's doctor, concerned about my own health, ordered me out of the training program for several weeks. Their concern was sincere, but it provided only a violent reaction in me—despite the knowledge that they feared that the pressure building about me might cause me to crack altogether.

Not even the promise of the stars themselves could keep me at home, where I died a thousand deaths, helpless to aid my child, watching him die slowly before my very eyes. How helpless can a man be before he can stand no more! The doctors who attended Igor were the finest of my country, but his malady defied them . . . and I could barely stand to come home, watching my son who no longer kicked his legs and laughed as his mother caressed his sensitive skin. Now, Igor lay quietly, almost as if in his unknowing mind he could sense the inevitable.

I tried desperately to fling myself into my work, to force out the sight of Igor, the sound of Tamara's quiet weeping, the realization of what was happening—what *would* happen. And my bitterness did not abate when I knew that, even as we prepared to begin the long journey into space, all the scientific brains and manpower and medical science of my country availed my son not at all.

Finally Igor found his blessed oblivion, and whatever pain our child experienced in his quiet suffering was gone forever.

My wife was stalked by a grief that seemed to tear her apart, and I hated myself savagely for my inability to reach her, to console Tamara. Never once did she utter a single word of what loomed hugely in her mind . . . . Never did she complain or refer to her own fear that in what awaited me in space, Tamara might know yet another death of her family.

One of the cosmonaut's wives asked Tamara to spend several weeks with her in the country; I begged her to go. I watched her leave by train, her face white and her eyes barely seeing what went on about her.

Nothing could be done now . . . except to hope that time would, as always, close the scars.

Shortly afterward, the grueling preparations of the cosmonauts for more than two years came to their close.

At a special meeting called by the Space Commission in Moscow, we received the news—at long last.

The first man to pilot the Vostok into space was Yuri Alexeevitch Gagarin.

As though from a distance, I heard the voice of the scientist droning on.

". . . Cosmonaut Number Two will be Gherman Stephanovitch Titov . . ."

The die was cast.

9. First of the Cosmonauts

The powerful hatch door closed smoothly and with a commanding sense of finality. As the inspecting engineers proclaimed that the hatch now stood secured, I stared upward for a long moment at the sleek metal skin of Vostok I. A sharp realization that this same metal would soon be bathed in the surging radiations of space seemed almost to overwhelm me. I tried to see through the thick steel and insulating surface of the spaceship to watch Yuri beyond those curving walls; I wanted to reach in and to help him. But Yuri remained alone and hidden from my sight in his new world of steel and energy, and I knew that at this same moment while I hesitated—frustrated and helpless in my desire to offer to him my own hands—he moved with speed, with care and precision as his moment of destiny rushed closer.

No longer could I help. Yuri Gagarin, close friend and fellow cosmonaut, now stood entirely on his own—bearing the tremendous responsibility not only of his nation and his planet, but actually of the entire race of man. These are not empty words. We *believed* this to be so. I have never met any of the astronauts of the United States, but not for a single moment do I doubt that we could literally translate our feelings into the languages of one another, and find we have long carried the same thoughts.

Around me there continued a flurry of activity as the engineers and technicians attended to their last-minute tasks. Then no one remained by the towering concrete and steel gantry except myself. I stood in the shadow of the great rocket, immersed in my thoughts of this wonderful moment of history, feeling a rich and deep rapport with my friend who lay surrounded by metal . . . anxious to rush where man had waited so long to travel.

Slowly I looked around me, held my gaze for a final long moment at mankind's first spaceship, and turned to leave. I walked as quickly as I could in the bulky space suit to the waiting bus. Several engineers reached out to support me as I climbed into the vehicle, but gratefully no one spoke. At this moment I wanted no words; I moved too deeply amid my own thoughts and emotions.

The bus braked to a halt outside the gaping doorway to the command post. I climbed down the steps, turned for a moment to look upward toward the deep blue sky, and then lumbered my way through the steel archway into the building. My steps felt unreal, for inside the helmet I could not hear the sound of my booted heels striking the floor. Inside the operations room a technician removed my helmet; I heard Yuri's voice as he chatted with an engineer about some item in the countdown. I stepped to the rear of the room where two technicians helped me to remove the bulky space suit, and I felt relief at leaving the brilliant orange coloring that made me stand out like a flashing neon light.

As I donned my uniform I studied the vast electronic control center, filled with row upon row of high banks of instruments. The center is almost impossible to describe; it is a neat and orderly procession of thousands of instrument dials and gauges, of gleaming control consoles, tape recorders, radar scopes and oscillographs. A thousand small sounds move through the room intermingled with the voices of the men who chant the calls of the countdown. And even when discipline is enforced—as it always is when the great booster rocket is alive and charged with its energy—there is an underlying, furious hum. My attention kept returning to a glass panel where the final minutes and seconds flashed away into the past, and Yuri's epochal moment rushed closer and closer.

At this moment I was no longer the standby spaceman to our nation's first cosmonaut. Until the moment that I began to remove the space suit, there was always that possibility, no matter how remote, that some emergency might demand my immediate return to the gantry to replace Yuri in his Vostok I. Fortunately that moment vanished, and from then on my role as an active participant in Yuri's flight was gone. I could relax—as much as any man can relax when his best friend is about to make the first space flight in history—and observe the proceedings as a spectator.

Long after those minutes in the command post were behind me, I was asked about my feelings when Yuri left the earth behind in an intense blaze of flaming energy. Was I disappointed? Or, perhaps, did I know a sensation of relief?

It is impossible to answer such a question; there really is no single answer. My feelings were a strange mixture of a thousand different emotions. Of course, I would have received gladly the honor to be the first of all men to lead the way into space; Yuri will live forever in history because of this distinction. But in equal honesty, when we all learned that the choice of Cosmonaut 1 had fallen on Yuri's shoulders, not one among us questioned the wisdom of that decision.

To describe Yuri properly is to search frantically for adjectives not shopworn by their use; my friend Yuri Gagarin is a person of exceptional merit and of many talents. His flashing wit and sharp intelligence obviously were deciding factors in his selection; his blunt honesty endeared him no less to all those who counted him proudly among their friends. The feeling of regret I experienced when his name, and not mine, was announced for the first space flight was more than tempered by my pleasure in seeing Yuri receive this singular honor. And never could a shred of displeasure have entered my own mind, for as his standby my selection as Cosmonaut 2 was made known to me.

From the moment that we were informed of our selections in the flight program of Project Vostok, Yuri and I were inseparable.

Neither of us hardly made a move without the other being present, and we became known to our colleagues as "the twins." The title was not entirely without foundation, for not only did I offer Yuri my complete support in his preparation for his flight, but my responsibilities dictated that I function as his alter ego. If something were to go wrong, if Yuri were to become ill or suffer some injury, I would have to step in immediately to assume his position. Never did this appear likely, but it was an essential safeguard that assured us of the first manned flight as scheduled.

Approximately one month before that scheduled date, we reached the final nuts-and-bolts phase in our preparations. On March 9, 1961, Spacecraft IV thundered upward from Baikonur and streaked into almost exactly what the scientists had programmed into the booster vehicle. By "almost exactly" I mean that the orbital heights achieved were as close to perfection as might be obtained, and the mission was flown just as we had hoped. At more than 17,000 miles per hour Spacecraft IV whipped into orbit with a point closest to the earth of 113.9 miles, soaring to the high point of orbit (apogee) of 154.5 miles. Aboard the spacecraft—it weighed 10,340 pounds with its test equipment and animals—was the thirteen-pound dog Chernushka, cages filled with guinea pigs, black mice, insects and plant seeds for a variety of space experiments. All pilot equipment was carried, and an anthropomorphic dummy of exactly Yuri's body dimensions and weight was strapped into the pilot's contour seat.

After orbiting the earth several times, a ground command signal flashed its message to the ship in space; the retro-rockets blazed and the heavy spaceship decelerated. Long minutes later, the tracking stations reported the unmanned spacecraft descending safely beneath its great parachutes—with the recovery forces already moving in to meet the ship as it touched the earth.

This was cheering news, but our spirits really soared when, sixteen days later, the launching pad alongside that used for Spacecraft IV flamed with the gases of another giant booster and Spacecraft V was on its way into orbit around the world. And again the control center rang with the cheers of success as the heavy ship raced about the earth in perfect orbit—from 111 to 150 miles above the surface. Once again a dog—Zvezdochka—was aboard for the flight, with other animals and elaborate test instruments. And once again the flight ended with a completely successful re-entry and recovery.

No better proof of the complete reliability of the rocket boosters, the spaceship, and its controls could be asked. We received the word that the third launching complex was ready, that the final preparations were being completed with Yuri's Vostok.

Actually, our confidence could not have been greater. The tests of March 9th and 25th were of spacecraft identical to that of Vostok I—but on February 4th and 12th Baikonur had rumbled to the echoing thunder of two other tremendous rockets. These boosters sent into orbit satellite payloads each weighing more than 14,000 pounds. While recovery was not attempted—since they were not prototypes of manned spacecraft—the booster rockets performed flawlessly.

So Yuri was able to look at four perfect successes with the five-ton Vostoks. The promise for his flight of April 12th—our fifth major space launching in a period of only nine weeks—could not have been better.

I was grateful—and for his reasons, Yuri was no less so—that our wives also had become the closest of friends. Tamara and Valya, especially in the gulf that I knew with my wife since the loss of our son, found much in each other for mutual strength. It would be in error to say that our wives regarded the forthcoming flights into space with the confidence and assurance that marked our own outlook. But at least, sharing their fears with each other, Yuri and I could leave for Baikonur knowing that no matter what happened, neither Tamara nor Valya would have to suffer that stark loneli-

ness and helplessness that we had known as Igor fought his losing
battle for life. In this we—Yuri and I—found upspoken but welcome comfort.

On April 8th, four days before the scheduled launch of Vostok
I, Yuri and I flew to Baikonur in a plane filled with scientists, engineers, government officials and Air Force officers. As always now,
we shared the same room, went through the same medical inspections, worked on the same equipment, studied the same charts, and
looked with equal intensity throughout the spaceship as it stood
far above the ground atop its powerful multistage rocket booster.

On the morning of April 12th, while the world lay quietly in
darkness, Yuri Gagarin and I awoke early. Outside the sky
stretched naked of clouds, revealing the heavens choked with stars.
It was a sight to delight the eyes, and for more than its asthetic
sense; that sky of clarity promised the green light for Yuri's mission.. We went through a brief but sharp medical examination, ate
and showered, then waited patiently while doctors taped medical
sensors to our bodies so that while on the ground they could read
the living medical story of a man in space, connected as were the
electrical lines from the sensors to radio transmitters.

Then the space suits went on, a laborious process requiring the
help of several technicians whose every move was made beneath
the sharp-eyed scrutiny of our doctors and engineers. We stood
patiently while the suits were tested for pressure seal, for their
electrical connections and a hundred other things. Then it was
time to go, and we walked from our quarters to the transfer bus
in a delightful April morning. Yuri sat in the first double seat, and
I directly behind him—two twins of space. The driver made the
trip cautiously, and quite without drama. The rocket towered
overhead, out of sight from the bus as we climbed down onto the
concrete of the launching complex.

We stood together for several seconds, two unearthly creatures
of pygmy size along the base of the rocket and the hulking mass

of the service tower. Finally there could be no waiting . . . *the* moment was here.

I turned to Yuri. "Well, my friend, so it really is happening . . . and to you, after all."

He grinned through his helmet, his teeth flashing in the shadow of the bulbous covering. "If you need any help, Yuri," I added with a laugh, "just send for us!"

We tried to put our arms over each others shoulders, but in our space suits we were clumsy and awkward, and we both roared with laughter as the helmets clanged together with a sharp ringing sound. The crowd of technicians and officers stood around, uncertain as to what they should do, while Yuri and I laughed at our own clumsiness. At the foot of the gantry stood the Chief Constructor, waiting with government officials. They called to Yuri, and I stood back as our first spaceman walked to the gantry elevator. He climbed the steps with the Chief Constructor, then turned to face the crowd of some fifty engineers and technicians who were completing their last-minute preparations. Yuri expressed his thanks for their devotion to the program. These were not empty words, and any man who is involved directly in the tremendously intricate process of preparing an enormous rocket for flight into space well understands the intricate coordination that is required. Yuri turned his eyes to mine; we looked steadily at one another. He lifted his arm to me, then turned and stepped through the door into the elevator. He was gone.

The people about me walked quickly to their final duties. Everyone, that is, but myself. For long minutes I stood quietly, looking upward as the elevator carried him smoothly to the top of the gantry. From where I stood I could just see the open hatch. The elevator stopped. Yuri, now a tiny figure in his brilliant orange space suit, stepped briskly from the lift and entered the Vostok. I waited, watching . . . then the hatch swung closed. Yuri was gone from sight; I returned to the control center . . .

The countdown moved along perfectly, everything happening in its proper sequence. I stood by the communications console; the technicial moved aside as I reached for the microphone.

"Yuri?"

"Yes, Gera . . . go ahead."

"Aren't you bored, just sitting there?"

Yuri's chuckle came through the console speaker. "Please, Gera . . . you are interrupting the music." He laughed.

I glanced upward at the screen of the television monitor. Yuri was strapped securely into his seat. He seemed comfortable and, despite his seeming ease, anxious to begin the flight—as certainly I would have been.

Ten minutes to go . . .

One after the other the red and amber lights of the control panels turned to green; one after the other the technicians at each panel nodded their assent as their instruments flashed to them the desired information.

Two minutes to go . . .

Everything was ready. The tracking ships in the Pacific five hundred miles northwest of Hawaii, and in the Atlantic off the coast of Africa were ready, their positions showing as lights on the global tracking chart. All recovery and rescue forces reported they were ready.

A planet-wide force waited.

The clock read exactly seven minutes past nine A.M. when the test conductor's finger stabbed down on the last button. An electronic sequencer flashed its final commands, and the monster rocket came alive. I stared at the television monitor scanning the base of the rocket; the scene disappeared in a raging surge of energy that flung itself madly in all directions. Thousands of feet away the gases flattened bushes.

Then she was up, moving with furious energy. From an ascent that seemed for a few moments almost stately, the giant gathered strength and with a contemptuous explosion of flame, it rejected the earth. Even deep within the earth we felt the control center vibrate slightly from that awesome display of energy. Outside the thick steel and concrete walls, sound waves hammered against the earth and rolled on and on for many miles over the country-side. I shifted my gaze to another monitor; the rocket was higher, seen from a steeper angle. On the glass the blazing fire took on the lines of a huge sapphire rushing into space. Suddenly, six miles high, there appeared magically in the heavens a thick streak of white; a broad band proclaiming that the rocket had pushed into the stratosphere, announcing its rise with the unmistakable sign of its condensation trail.

Higher and higher, faster and faster! Long before the flame was out of our sight the booster was responding to its electronic masters, bending over from the vertical, moving toward a more horizontal line of ascent.

Then a new sound, and wonderful . . . . Yuri's voice, coming through the loudspeakers, clear despite the building forces of ac-celeration: "I see the earth in haze . . . . My, it is beautiful."

We all stood rooted to the spot, waiting for the fuel to be con-sumed, transformed into the now-violet flames gushing through vacuum. The word came in finally—cut off. The booster was at that instant traveling horizontal to the surface of the earth. This was *the* moment. Valves snapped shut; the flame died. Explosive bolts fired; then tiny scarlet tongues of flame lashed the vacuum— I could see every sequence in my mind—and Vostok I pushed away from the empty booster.

The radios hummed: *"Ya kharashom nastroyeniyii. Machina rabotayet kharasho . . ."* "I am in good spirits. The machine works perfectly . . ."

Relief washed through my body. In the control room the tech-nicians and engineers all wore tremendous smiles; some men clasped their hands over their heads in a silent gesture of triumph.

It had happened; it had *really* happened.

A human being was in orbit about the planet Earth. A man,

Yuri Gagarin, cosmonaut, my friend, at that same instant was flashing through the vacuum of space with a velocity of five miles every second . . . .

Three hundred miles to complete a sentence . . .

The wonder of it all!

General Kamanin walked up to me. "Titov . . . there's nothing we can do here now. Come, let's fly to the landing area; perhaps we can be there in time to meet Yuri when he lands."

Grateful for the offer, I rushed quickly to his airplane, waiting on the airstrip with its engines already turning over and ready for take off. We climbed into the airplane behind the pilots, quickly placing earphones to our heads, listening to the Vostok frequency. I never knew when the airplane's wheels lifted from the runway, so intently did I listen for every word, every sound.

"Feeling wonderful . . . . Can see earth, forests, clouds . . ." He was weightless; in his first few minutes of orbit Yuri had been weightless for a greater sustained period than had any man before him.

The radio remained silent for several minutes. I glanced down at the earth. Below us, the Kazakh steppes slid slowly beneath the speeding airplane.

" . . . flight still proceeding normally. Still feeling fine. Equipment faultless . . ."

Through space the Vostok hurtled, soundless, invisible to us, rushing around its mother world at nearly 18,000 miles per hour. I glanced at my watch; Yuri would soon plunge from daylight into nighttime, and would then emerge back into daylight before he was in position to approach his landing area. As I listened, I tensed as Yuri's voice abruptly took on a note of aggravation. Then I laughed . . . . His equipment still worked perfectly, but while taking notes Yuri had apparently released his grip on his pencil and it floated away from him, out of reach!

At ten-thirty I was as nervous as a cat; the general stared at me until I pointed at my wristwatch. He nodded in understanding.

Yuri was now rushing toward the most critical time of his mission—the point where he must begin to re-enter the earth's atmosphere. If anything went wrong here . . . then Yuri Gagarin would disappear forever in a long blaze of white fire that would never again touch the surface of the world. I closed my eyes, in my mind seeing everything that happened the way I hoped it was happening.

Exactly at thirty-five minutes past ten o'clock Vostok I flashed through vacuum over Central Africa. By now, having received final instructions and data from the Atlantic tracking ships for orientation and timing, Yuri had adjusted his controls. The reaction jets swung Vostok into the proper attitude for retro-fire . . .

One hundred and twenty miles above Africa and 4,500 miles from its destination, Vostok I began the process of starting home. An automatic timer clicked. The retros sent fiery gases splattering into vacuum, then winked out. Vostok now fell around the earth with several hundred miles per hour of her speed gone. That was enough. If all was going well, Yuri was on his way back to us.

Descending in a giant arc, Vostok would begin to glow a deep red color. This would deepen to a bright red, and then a frightening yellow-orange as friction with the air heated the metal surface of the spaceship to thousands of degrees. Inside, strapped down in his contour seat, I could almost see Yuri bearing the forces of deceleration that stood like a monster talon on and about his body . . . .

For ten minutes we heard nothing, and then came the words from Yuri himself that brought a chorus of cheers ringing through our airplane. A bit weak and breathless, Yuri called out that he was through the atmosphere, his parachutes had deployed, he was coming down slowly, safely—in triumph! The general and I pounded one another on our backs and hugged each other in sheer exuberance. Our relief was indescribable, our joy beyond description.

Exectly one hour and forty-eight minutes after his booster rockets ignited with their flash of fire, Yuri Gagarin stood again on the

firm surface of his planet. Vostok I descended to earth in a cultivated field near the village of Smedlovka, about four hundred
miles southeast of Moscow.

Exactly where it was intended to land.

Yuri was on the ground before our wheels again touched a runway, and we listened breathlessly by radio as we heard his words
reporting directly to Premier Khruschev of the success of his flight.
I could just imagine the scene back at our training center in Moscow where the other cosmonauts were receiving the news even as
we did. There would be some sore backs and aching muscles from
all the fists pounding in jubilation!

The pilot radioed ahead for staff cars to be ready and waiting
for us; scarcely had the plane screeched to a halt than we were
outside and climbing into the vehicles. Soldiers had brought Yuri
to an Army post close by his landing point, and we braked to a
stop at the edge of a growing crowd of farmers, soldiers, generals
and scientists. Heedless of military rank or courtesy I fought my
way through the mob, using my elbows and arms freely to shove
my way to the front. Yuri saw me emerge from the throng and
broke off a report to a scientist in mid-sentence. He rushed to me
and for the second time that morning we embraced. Our excitement was so great we could barely talk to one another, and settled
instead for enthusiastic back-slapping and cries of laughter.

Finally I managed to get through my excitement to a question
about the flight. Yuri's laughter died abruptly. His face became
serious, but his eyes gleamed as he looked into mine.

"Gera . . . my friend, it is beyond all description. It is beautiful
beyond words. To see with your own eyes . . . for the first time,
Gera . . . the spherical shape of the earth."

Yuri Gagarin, only minutes returned to his own world, already
longed to return to the space beyond . . . .

10. Countdown for Vostok II

Yuri Gagarin's return to Moscow signaled two major events to begin: the tumultuous welcome of all Moscow and the country for the world's first man in space and, less obvious to the public eye, the preparations for the flight of Vostok II. The celebrations were wonderful, but our own participation because of the tight security rein on the project was limited to gatherings behind the scenes. Which was just as well—I simply had no time for celebrations. Although we sorely missed him in our preparations—for his counsel was invaluable—Yuri's departure for visits to the different countries of the world closed the door on much of the outside interference that had begun to accumulate irritatingly about our small group.

But before he left we spent wonderful moments with Yuri. As quickly as he could leave the doctors and the scientists who asked thousands of questions of him, Yuri joined his cosmonaut friends. The hours disappeared quickly as Yuri told us in the smallest detail of what his trip had been like, of the wonders of the earth from space, of his pleasant reactions to weightlessness.

He said that the effect of zero gravity, while not totally unexpected because of his brief periods of weightlessness in aircraft, felt "somewhat unusual" to him. But he "quickly became accustomed to this sensation of weightlessness, adapted myself to this situation, and continued to carry out the program . . ."

In orbit, Yuri ate food and drank liquids from the special containers placed in Vostok with him. He took notes, and warned me to hold the pad securely in one hand while I wrote with the other. He laughed as he explained his astonishment at watching the pencil float away from his hand after forgetting for a moment to keep a tight grasp on any object in the weightless spaceship.

His arms and legs, he said, felt unusual—but strange—for some minutes because of their total lack of weight. This did not present any problems to him, and actually made easier the work he had to do in the cabin. He watched a globe that was synchronized to rotate with the movement of Vostok. In case of an emergency, Yuri had before him at all times an "optical orientator" mounted by one of the portholes. This consisted of two circular mirror reflectors, a light filter, and a periscope with a grid. As Vostok followed its course, Yuri observed the horizon image as a ring in his field of vision. He checked the orientation of Vostok's longitudinal axis by watching the "travel" of the earth's surface, and he had controls which would turn the spaceship so that the horizon line could be seen in the orientator in the form of a concentric ring, and the direction of "travel" of the earth's surface would coincide with the course line of the grid.

On his flight Yuri did many work assignments—his flight lasted from beginning to end exactly 108 minutes, including his time in orbit of 89.1 minutes—of this total he was weightless for seventy minutes. It was during this interval that Yuri ate and drank, wrote notes, worked a telegraph key, monitored his instruments and other equipment, and monitored his automatic control system. As Vostok raced from daylight into darkness and then shot back into daylight again, a solar orientation system flicked on. One axis of Vostok was aligned with the sun through optical and gyroscopic instruments. These transmitted signals to the control system which, in turn, commanded the control devices to stabilize the spaceship according to the flight plans programmed into the ship's electronic brain—the auto-pilot.

Although at any time of the flight Yuri could take over control and manually direct the attitude of his craft, as well as its point of re-entry, he did none of these things. We preferred the first manned flight to be essentially a test of the man himself under the conditions of space—it was not a test of the Vostok, as such. The spaceship had orbited the earth enough times in perfect success to assure all concerned that its automatic systems presented no problems.

But the most fascinating stories Yuri had to relate to us were his impressions of the flight, of space and the earth. He regretted that his flight through the "night side" of the planet took place mostly over the oceans, so that no cities appeared beneath him—pools of light that he was most anxious to see from space. At the southernmost part of his orbit he shot past Antarctica, two thousand miles below Santiago, Chile. He flashed past Cape Horn, burst through the darkness into dawn, and witnessed a sight that hypnotized him for several minutes.

"When I emerged from the shadow of the earth, the horizon looked different . . . There was a bright orange strip along it which passed into a blue hue and once again into a dense black color."

He explained that at any time "the view of the horizon is quite unique and . . . it is very beautiful. It is possible to see the remarkably colorful change from the light surface of the earth to the completely black sky in which one can see the stars.

"This dividing line is very thin, just like a belt of film surrounding the earth's sphere, a film like a narrow belt girdling the globe. It is of a soft light blue color and the entire transition from blue to black is most smooth and beautiful. . . ."

We begged him to go on.

"I did not see the moon. The sun . . . well, it's tens of times brighter than we see it here. The stars are bright and distinct; they're really quite visible. And the entire picture of the sky . . . of the firmament presents much more contrast than when seen from the earth . . ."

He described to us his ability to distinguish landmarks such as rivers, mountains, cities and other features, and then returned to a description of the earth and space itself.

"There's a very characteristic and very beautiful blue halo about the earth," he said. "The aureole becomes distinct at the horizon when gradual transition in colors takes place from soft blue light, from light blue to blue, dark blue, violet to black, to a quite black sky. When emerging from the earth's shadow . . . the sun fell on and penetrated the atmosphere. At this point the halo took on a slightly different color . . .

"On the surface itself, on the very horizon of the surface, I could see a bright orange color, which then merged into all the colors of the rainbow, giving light blue, deep blue, violet and black colors to the sky. There is simply nothing like it here on earth. . . ."

That much I knew—now. And if all went well, it might not be too long before Yuri and I could compare our notes of our planet from the vantage of space.

Before that would happen, several critical assignments required immediate attention. And as the secretly assigned pilot for Vostok II, it was urgent that I coordinate many of the new modifications for the spaceship with the detailed schedule of the entire mission. This required me to attend meetings at instrument laboratories, tracking stations, propulsion centers, workshops and other indus-trial-technical-scientific locations. With Yuri's flight behind us, we had—to beggar the cliché—one foot now solidly on the ground for continued flight in space.

The news that I would orbit the earth for more than seventeen times stunned and delighted me. More than twenty-five hours for the mission!

Our preparations differed sharply from those for Vostok I, since we now were specifically to seek out extensive data on the prac-ticable aspects of the flight. Yuri's mission can never be matched simply because it was the first and, to some extent, we moved with a necessary wedge of caution. Much of that reserve could now be dissolved in light of the superb reactions of Yuri himself, and the unprecedented reliability of the rocket boosters and the spacecraft.

We found no need for changes in certain essential items. The life-support system that substituted for the earth itself could not have performed better. Cabin pressure, atmospheric constituents, temperature—all of these items worked perfectly. The system to absorb exhaled gases from the cabin air also functioned exactly as planned.

But there still were changes to be made; no matter how insignificant they might be, they were important to our flight. The changes improved the pilot's capabilities for observation or his comfort in essential form; after talking with Yuri, I requested additional monitoring and navigation instruments in the spaceship. The scientists were already installing their own equipment necessary to meet the requirement for seventeen orbits.

The need for improved pilot visibility through the spaceship gave me added window space. Yuri carried no camera, but I would bring along with me a Konvass, a small hand camera used widely by newsmen. There was a new instrument called a *zritel*—or viewer—through which I would be able to pick out individual cities on the earth. This gave me a choice of magnification of three to five times normal. It would enable me to see Moscow, for example; not Red Square itself, but nevertheless there would be no mistaking the entire city.

With me at all times as I worked on the designs of the spaceship, as I continued my minimum one-hour daily routine of hard calisthenics, as I flew from base to base, as I sat for hours in the simulator devices . . . with me at all times was Cosmonaut 3. Just as I worked as Yuri's alter ego for the flight of Vostok I, so my standby cosmonaut lived almost as my shadow, helping, watching, always ready to slip right into my place as I was ready to do the same with Yuri.

It is regrettable that he cannot be identified at this time. One of my closest friends, he is the calmest man in an emergency that I have ever known, and his solid-rock look upon the worst of disasters (even when he personally is involved) is a subject of much discussion among the scientists and doctors. Once he flew a powerful jet fighter—damaged and flaming—to a safe forced landing without power, when it seemed absolutely impossible that he could even survive. He walked away without a scratch, already noting down on a pad in the most precise engineering terms what had gone wrong with the machine. He speaks so seldom that when he does talk, we all listen to every word—invariably his rare sentences result from careful, long thinking.

Working with me as closely as it was necessary to do so, he came to know Vostok II as well as I did. In one sense he knew even more, for through all our work he took notes constantly on the spaceship in which he would make his mission—Vostok III.

[*I believe it to be of especial importance to interrupt Titov's narrative here to emphasize a point especially relating to the flight of Vostok II. Nowhere in his notes does Major Titov relate in any fashion to the design, flight, research with, and future of Vostok II as anything more than a major research and scientific vehicle. Obviously this is to be expected. And our own Department of Defense, through the office of Secretary Robert McNamara, enhances this "purely scientific effort" with the incredible viewpoint, expressed officially, that the flight of Vostok II was no more than another step forward in the Soviet's "peaceful exploration of space."*

This is a blind and a ridiculous premise; it is, to me, a frightening exhibition to observe, so grimly reminiscent of past occasions when we deluded ourselves that others in the world lack a hard, practical nature.

Every shred of evidence we can obtain points more and more clearly to the fact that the Russians are not so foolish as to create artificial barriers between their scientific research and their anticipated military needs in space—something of which we ourselves are guilty.

It seems clear beyond all doubt that Vostok II is a hard and practical research tool of the Russian military manned space program. Nowhere does Titov mention the external control surfaces of his heavy spaceship—but these external surfaces exist, and they permitted Titov a limited, but definite, manual control of his spaceship during re-entry into the earth's atmosphere, and a definite control of his vehicle during the descent through the lower atmosphere. This allows the pilot considerable latitude in selecting his landing area, or in overcoming re-entry errors. It is interesting to note that the limited control surfaces of Vostok II are predecessors of equipment already being designed into OUR own future spaceships.

Vostok II—unlike Gagarin's ship—mounted two stub wings jutting from its midsection to permit limited atmospheric control. And similar to Gagarin's ship, Vostok II mounted a tail annulus, which featured a row of small moving shutters or flaps. Engineering studies reveal that with this equipment, Vostok II in 1961 would have more extensive pilot control than would our own two-man Gemini spaceship (two tons lighter than Vostok) when that vehicle flies in 1964. (MARTIN CAIDEN)|

We worked under the shadow of a cloud during the final preparations for my flight—a shadow that was invisible to us, not of earth, and yet that contained great potential danger. Because of the time I was programmed to remain in space, astronomers checked carefully every hour of the day the intensity of eruptions and storms on the surface of the sun—ninety-three million miles distant from my scheduled orbit. Yet the caution was well grounded. Two weeks before the scheduled launch the sun cast forth a spectacular storm; a vast cloud of solar radiation rushed invisibly through space and swept across the earth. A man in the path of that electrical violence might well have been flooded with damaging radiations. But the astronomers passed on the reassuring word that the sun would not cast any of its violence toward the earth during my scheduled orbiting, and that the flight could proceed as scheduled.

Impatiently, we completed our schedule of tasks at the Moscow training center, at the various industrial sites around the country. When we received the welcome news that the spaceship was enroute to Baikonur, we knew that the final phase of the preparations was upon us. Shortly after Vostok II arrived at the launch site to be mated with the booster rocket, I left with Cosmonaut 3 for Baikonur.

Things were not the same as they had been for Yuri's flight. I was surprised to discover that as the man assigned to the actual space mission there was surprisingly little for me to do, and that everyone else staggered under their assignments. I had time—for which I was thankful—to watch the work under way on the great booster rockets, to chat idly with the ground staff and the engineers, to study the tracking equipment. I talked to the emergency fire and rescue crews, and made idle jokes with them about my hopes that they would have absolutely nothing to do when the time came for me to leave them.

At the command post underground, where I watched Yuri's own launching, I noticed major changes and alterations in the control center. The experience of Yuri's single orbit was enough to dictate improvements, and several large new electronic machines and consoles had been added to the room. Of course . . . some of the changes were required by the need for at least three shifts of technicians—one on duty, one sleeping, and the third always standing by.

The days fled—distressingly slow, and yet they seemed to vanish without my being aware of their passing. And then it was the last afternoon, the last evening before the mission—the final night of sleep on the earth.

Lunch proved to be healthy, but unsatisfying, since both myself and the standby cosmonaut were required to eat only from the "joyless tubes" of space food. After lunch, the expected medical check, and then several hours simply to catch up on the many small details that must be attended to.

Several writers and photographers from *Tass* were waiting for a conference—they remained discreetly in the background at all times until we were free to talk with them without interruption—to record last minute impressions. After out meeting I made it clear that for the rest of the day I did not wish to be disturbed any further for this purpose, and retired to my room—alone—to write a long letter to Tamara. With this out of the way I felt relaxed, and went for a long walk with my standby cosmonaut.

Our conversation touched gently on many subjects rather than the hard technical requirements of the flight. What had to be done, was done by now. I knew full well how the man with me felt; not so long ago I had been in his same position as I walked along-side Yuri, while he waited for his countdown to move toward the moment of actual firing. We discussed the weather, the look of the countryside in late summer, our families and our friends; casual and relaxing conversation. My standby told me as we walked back toward our quarters that we were invited this night to dine with our two doctors—Yevgeni Anatolovitch and Andrei Victorovitch; unfortunately, "dinner" for us consisted of the same space food squeezed unceremoniously from their tubes.

I have been unfair in my neglect of these two men. Anatolovitch and Victorovitch were more than our doctors; they were our mentors, our brothers, our teachers. They looked after us with a care that not even a mother could have criticized, and nothing we did was without their careful observation, their assistance and deep friendship.

In mid-afternoon I returned with my standby to the little wood and concrete house—"Cosmonaut's Cottage"—where I had slept once before on the eve of a manned space flight. I would sleep again in the same bed, and my standby cosmonaut in Yuri's. My pajamas were neatly laid out, late newspapers and magazines waited on a low table, and pinned to my pillow was the detailed timetable for the morning. Of all the pieces of paper I found to be unnecessary, this one was it—I knew the schedule in my mind down to the last second.

There were still several hours before it was time to retire, and I could not sit still reading magazines. I drove to the launch pad and rode the elevator in the gantry up to Vostok for a final check-out of the spaceship. I could not help stopping for a moment to admire the enormous rocket looming upward from the ground; it gleamed under its brilliant spotlights, festooned with cables and protective cocooning in its more vital areas, where control and guidance equipment were located.

Atop the rocket, high above the ground, the wind blew strong and cold. I squeezed through the square doorway into the cabin; abruptly the outside noise faded out and I was once again completely content. *This* was home to me; I knew every square inch of the spaceship. Every part was functional, and yet every part shone with a beauty that never failed to deeply impress me. I eased into the pilot's seat, relaxing until I felt completely comfortable. My hand moved lightly over the instrument console, and idly I flicked the intercom switch that linked the ship to ground control. I thought the lines to be closed, but instantly I heard, "Yes, sir?" I smiled; no one was leaving anything to chance tonight.

"Testing, testing," I called back, feeling like a little boy caught with his hand in the cookie jar. But the command post radio technicians were pleased that I was in the spaceship; while I was already there, would I mind assisting them in a final check-out— for the thousandth time, I imagined, for them—of the system? It was nearly an hour later before silence fell once more in the cabin.

I looked around, slowly, critically. Nothing was amiss; everything was perfect. I left the capsule carefully, almost as if I were trying to avoid disturbing the feeling of quiet and wonder that filled the cabin. At the bottom of the elevator, as I stepped out onto the gantry platform, I was startled to see the Chief Constructor, standing with several engineers.

I clasped his hand warmly. He smiled as I told him of that final hour in the capsule, of my feelings. We drove back to the cottage, with a promise from the engineer to meet with me after dinner.

The meal went quietly, with Cosmonaut 3 showing a growing excitement with the passing hours—quite unlike him! I wondered if I were being *too* subdued in my own reactions, but my feelings were of complete contentment in everything that had been done, and I felt as if excitement on my own part now would simply be out of place. I was simply . . . waiting.

I asked the doctors if they knew where Yuri was at this moment; even as I voiced the question, I realized that something *was* indeed missing. I wished that Yuri could have been present, could have been with me as I was with him before his own flight.

"He is in Canada tonight," one doctor replied. "It's all part of the trip he has been making around the world, as ordered by Moscow . . . " No denying my disappointment at his absence. Canada seemed such a tremendous distance from Baikonur. I felt Yuri separated from me in time as well as in space. It was possible— even likely—that he did not even know that the launching date was tomorrow. Anyway, he would know soon enough.

As promised, the Chief Constructor arrived shortly after dinner, waiting patiently while the doctors made their final medical checks for the day. Later we walked together along the springy turf of the airstrip perimeter, with Cosmonaut 3 by my side, both of us listening attentively to the engineer's final words and suggestions. "Above all, Titov," he said, "remember that you will be the first to fly with the manual control system. We know it is effective . . . but I wish you to be cautious in your first control attempts. Be thorough in what you do, and bear in mind that you may need to use the manual system in the event of an emergency.

Especially if you are forced to re-enter somewhere else besides the assigned landing place . . . Then the manual control will mean everything to you."

He paused as a meteor flashed silently against the evening sky, leaving behind it a faint trace like a diamond scratch on dark blue glass. A pale, crescent moon hung in the skies, bringing with it a rapid fall of darkness.

The engineer glanced at his watch, and laid his hand on my shoulder. "Sleep well. Your day is going to be twenty-five hours long tomorrow."

The doctors waited patiently for us in the cottage. Yevgenie Anatolovitch started a game of chess with my standby; I rested in my bunk, staring at the ceiling, my thoughts far from Baikonur. Far indeed; they were out of this world.

At ten o'clock we undressed. The doctors taped eight medical sensors to each of our bodies and connected them with recorders on the side of the room. Thirty minutes later we were both asleep. The last sounds I heard before dropping off were faint metallic clangs that drifted to the cottage from the launch site. They rang clearly but gently in the night.

11. Final Moments

I awoke to the light touch of a hand on my chest. I looked up at Doctor Anatolovitch, who smiled: "Not sleeping late, are you . . . today of all days?" I grinned at him and threw off the covers. The doctor leaned down to quickly disconnect the medical sensors.

I fairly jumped from the bed to the floor—and stopped short. The room smelled sweet; during the night someone had taken the trouble to place on our bureau a large vase filled with roses still wet from the night dew. I walked quickly to the window and looked out, a fighter pilot's old habit in the morning. Outside the world could not have been more beautiful. The sky shone clearly, and a golden sun was just breaking the horizon.

"Good morning, Gera!" Cosmonaut 3 stood by my side, equally grateful for the perfect weather. "You've got just the right conditions—wonderful." Aside from this one remark, he said not another word about the flight that was now only a few hours away. Our conversation remained on everyday, trivial items as we went through the final medical examination.

Again everything took place with a sense of familiarity; I had followed this identical routine when I played the role of standby cosmonaut for Yuri's flight. My thoughts were very much on that day as well as for my own ascent into space. Together, Cosmonaut 3 and I went through the usual calisthenics, and then ate our

157

breakfast from the same type of bronzed tubes that were already stored in Vostok II. Then we prepared for the actual flight.

First the doctors taped new medical sensors to our skin. After this they assisted me in donning the white woolen thermal underwear. I slipped into the lightweight blue nylon inner suit. Then my socks. Technicians moved forward to assist me in putting on the brilliant orange space suit that trailed electrical leads, later to be hooked up in the spaceship cabin. Experienced attendants checked every move and helped me along every step of the way. They secured my boots and used special care in placing the white helmet over my head, locking it tightly to the space suit's neck ring.

Within an hour of being awakened, I was ready to leave the cottage for the launching pad. We shuffled our way through the cottage and climbed into the cream-and-blue bus waiting outside; my standby sat directly behind me, as I had sat behind Yuri only four months before. We grinned at one another, but said nothing. Words were unnecessary, and we each were deep in our own thoughts.

The road stretched far ahead of the bus, a long paved line moving through sun drenched fields, filled with wildflowers, on either side of the road. Then, around a turn, past a grove of trees—and there it was.

High above the ground, shining in the sun, towering over everything else on Baikonur, my rocket waited. Around it stood the latticed metal gantry, still filled with technicians ending their countdown tasks. Even as we approached in the bus, I knew that dozens of men were already walking away from their work towers, their jobs completed.

And above all else, the spaceship waited for her pilot.

We climbed down from the bus. I turned to the friend who had stood so long and so well at my side, supporting me during my preparations for the flight. "Well, so it is really *I* who am going!" I said.

He flashed a smile through his helmet. "Good luck to you, Gera." We clasped each other about the shoulders and, as had happened once before, I broke out laughing as our helmets clanged together. We simply weren't used to embracing in space suits, but it was fast becoming a tradition among the exclusive fraternity of cosmonauts. Perhaps it's the metallic clamor of the helmets that speeds a man on his way.

I started to say something to him, but at that moment another bus pulled up and out spilled the rest of the cosmonauts. They formed a circle. Each man threw his arms about me and for a moment hugged me tightly. Each had the same message, the same two words.

"Good flight!"

The feeling of elation and anticipation around the base of the launching platform was almost a live and tangible thing. The morning was beautiful; birds sang in the brush just beyond the concrete pad; broad smiles showed everywhere. This was no first flight . . . . With Yuri's sensational success before me, and four perfect robot flights immediately before that, my chances could not have been better. The countdown proceeded without a single moment of major trouble; minor difficulties were disposed of almost as quickly as they came up.

Standing on the side of the cosmonaut group was the Chairman of the State Commission, to whom I reported officially that I was prepared to begin the flight. A civilian, he replied to my terse military report to him by grasping my gloved hand in his own hand and smiling, "Comrade Titov . . . our hearts go with you." Whatever official ceremony he had come to fulfill . . . he completely ignored it!

I climbed the iron steps to the stand where the elevator gate stood open, waiting for me. I turned to address the engineers, pad workers, the technicians and doctors, the cosmonauts; as I spoke briefly to them I stared into the eyes of the Chief Constructor, who stood silently on the side. For my final words I formally dedicated my mission in space to the Twenty-second Congress. My words would be flashed to Moscow even before I left.

Abruptly I turned and entered the elevator. It rose slowly, each additional second revealing to me more and more of the sweep of the countryside. I stepped from the elevator on the platform leading to the spaceship. But first, for a long moment, I looked down at the tremendous rocket that would carry me away from the earth. I listened to the sounds of life that hissed and growled from the hundreds of tons of metal and fuel. Then I held both hands over my head in a final salute to the little group watching me from far below, and turned to the waiting spaceship.

Inside, I eased into my seat and secured my straps and hoses. All electrical connections made and secured—good. That was all for the moment. I reached out and depressed a switch.

The hatch door closed behind me smoothly, without a sound. I was alone with the instruments; one flashed the signal that the hatch was sealed and locked.

The great trial was about to begin, and I felt, finally, at home, where I belonged. Everything was so richly familiar to me. Switches, buttons, dials . . . and a magnificent colored globe of the planet that would rotate in unison with the oceans and continents soon to rotate under my spaceship and indicate to me, precisely, where I was at any given moment over the surface of the world below.

I ran my hands swiftly across the controls and the instruments. I stared at a bank of instruments, then scanned the flickering needles in front of the luminous dials. Before me there glowed softly the colors of red, yellow, green on the color indicator panel.

I snapped out of the feelings into which I had fallen. Time enough in the past—and in the future—to contemplate with such emotion the wonder that I knew lay behind these instruments. I clamped a firm discipline upon my mind, and set about my preflight checklists with the thoroughness for which I had been trained.

But even as I worked my thoughts drifted . . . . I had thought often in the past, and did so again now, of the ordeal of the first astronaut of our competitors. One of the doctors told me that Commander Shepard had slept for only a few brief hours prior to his suborbital flight. Like the other cosmonauts and members of our program, we read the detailed reports forwarded to us from the Space Commission in Moscow of Shepard's preparations, his countdown and his flight. I knew that because of the interruptions in his countdown, the man had spent nearly five hours in his small capsule before his launching.

Five hours—a very grueling ordeal! The competition as reported by the news correspondents may be severe, and there may be international complications involved, but every time that I thought of the American astronaut in that capsule as the hours dragged by, I felt only sympathy for him. Yuri had known a countdown that moved exactly on schedule, and I enjoyed the same kind of precision that required my presence in the capsule prior to launch for only the minimum required time.

Had the count been delayed, there would have been no discomfort. As spacious and as comfortable as a small, well-furnished room, the cabin was also easy on the eyes with soft luminescent lights. I could recline far back, sit almost upright, work, or even sleep in the white plastic seat with its deep-cushion feeling. It was actually like a well-padded deck chair, perfectly contoured to my body. The bearings mounting permitted the seat to adjust to the angle I desired, as well as changing automatically during flight when acceleration or deceleration forces varied.

Everything lay within easy reach of my hands and vision. From the sitting or reclining position I watched every dial and every color indicator. I could look easily through the porthole; touch every button, switch, handle; talk comfortably with the earth stations by radiophone and, in an emergency, use the telegraph key; and it was easy enough to make entries in the spaceship's log, which I would be required to do during each hour of flight that I was awake.

I breathed air that was cleaner than any room in any home. The pressure within the cabin remained the same as at sea level, with the same constituents, but it was cleansed thoroughly by the Vostok's life-support system. Simply by turning knobs within my reach I could adjust humidity, pressure, and the cabin temperature.

Alongside the rotating globe of the planet—about five inches in diameter—was the world's most unique speedometer. Within a small black rectangle I would see the registering of white figures, not in miles or kilometers, but in the number of revolutions and decimal points of revolutions around the earth. It is awesome to realize the message that it displays.

I had only to flick a switch, and then allow the fingers of my right hand to close over a polished black handle. With this handle —the space counterpart of a fighter pilot's control stick—I could actually "fly" the spaceship in orbit. Such flight is only in respect to attitude changes; the movement of the handle in turn causes reaction jets to fire in space, changing the spaceship's attitude in terms of yaw, pitch and roll. It is impossible to change orbit or to deflect from orbit within a major source of energy, and even the superb Vostok was not yet at this stage of development.

The manual control fitted neatly into my clenched fist. There was a groove for each finger and a small white button beneath my thumb. A small instrument with which to control a five-ton mass hurtling along at five miles every second!

I contacted Ground Control in the operations center control room; they ordered the instrument and controls check-out coordinated with their panels to begin at once. With the small number of instruments and devices in the cabin—much less, as stated before, than in a jet fighter—this required only several minutes.

Strange, but all sense of excitement had left me. Even with my intent to concentrate precisely upon my duties, I thought I would maintain an undercurrent of emotion. But it fled completely; I am not one of those individuals of iron will who can switch his emotions on and off like an electric light at any given moment. It was more than this....

I enjoyed absolute confidence in Vostok, in the great rockets standing below me, in the men who were responsible from the ground for my success and my safety. I knew the Vostok spaceship so thoroughly I could not have had a better knowledge of the craft had I already lived in it for years. I believed in its reliability and that of its systems even more than I believed myself capable to conduct the mission as it was designed to be carried out.

No human frailties could interfere with the performance of the spaceship. Everything to do with its operation in space, and during the re-entry into the atmosphere had been calculated with such precision that never would I wonder at any given moment as to my own duties. The scheduled program in space was of course to be complicated and exacting.

This did not cause any apprehension. I was trained to a razor's edge, observed by the finest doctors, and my performance considered as good as humanly possible by scientists who had the most extensive space flight experience and knowledge in the world. The performance of our rockets preceding my own flight, the tremendous mission flown by Yuri Gagarin . . . all these things and more led to an emotional state in which I felt absolutely calm.

During the countdown checklist, I had several moments in which to talk to the other cosmonauts who had crowded into the control center. I could picture them standing around the television monitors, just as I had done for Yuri's flight . . . and probably just as tense and nervous as I had been then, while Yuri relaxed in Vostok I, his absolute sense of confidence permitting him to listen to music!

No—they were more confident now of the success of my flight, with the shining star of Yuri's single orbit behind us to dispel our fears of weightlessness and other problems. One of the cosmonauts reminded me of the time when I became snarled in a corkscrew dive during parachute training. He warned me to return to earth this time in a more gentle fashion, or else I would be requested to leave the private club of the cosmonauts; I could hear their laughter in the control room, and imagine the unsmiling face of the test conductor, who had never tolerated any levity in *his* program!

Then someone in the control center did me a great personal favor. In my earphones, as a background to our conversation, I heard the same song we had played while Yuri waited for his countdown to end . . . and thoughts of his own flight rushed back to me in a flood, until the test conductor broke in to concentrate upon the next sequence of checklist events instead of the music.

I had been sealed into Vostok II for twenty minutes when a red oblong signal light suddenly flashed. From this second on there was no more time for levity, or for music. The time on my clock showed exactly fifty minutes past eight—only ten minutes to go. The first of the six hundred remaining seconds disappeared as the sweep hand of the chronometer rolled around the face of the dial.

For the last time I went through the checklist as the test conductor called out his signals and his commands. In the blockhouse the amber and red lights winked out, and green flashed in their place. We were closer and closer. From this point on I would receive voice contact only when we progressed to another action sequence in the countdown. I heard the voices of the control center calling out the readiness reports of the worldwide tracking stations, the airborne search and recovery teams ready to race after me in the event of a premature re-entry anywhere about the world, the vast assembly of thousands and thousands of men all coordinating their activities down to the final moment.

Another voice . . . the Chariman of the State Commission, offering me for all the people of the Soviet Union his best wishes for my mission.

The second hand swept around and around. . . .

Three minutes to go.

My calmness vanished as though a whirlwind roared through my body and my mind. I could feel my body tense as the seconds flashed by, one after the other. I knew Yuri's medical reports by heart . . . in these last minutes his pulse increased from 67 to 132. I could not tell my own of course; later the doctors watching the medical monitoring panels in the control center told me that my own pulse had shot up to exactly that registered for Yuri at the same moment.

I knew none of this at the time; only that my body was semi-rigid, my mind terribly sharp and clear . . . impatient for the seconds to flee . . .

A voice broke in: *"Sixty seconds and counting . . ."*

My lips moved without sound, counting of their own accord . . . *"Twenty . . . nineteen . . . eighteen . . ."*

Deep in the bowels of the enormous rocket, machinery came alive. A groan shuddered through the giant.

My eyes stayed glued to the chronometer, to that sweep hand gliding around . . .

"Eight . . . seven . . . six . . ."

I braced myself; my fingers squeezed around the arm rests. The sweep hand was coming upright now . . .

"Three . . . two . . ."

The needle stood upright.

I heard the firing command: *"Natchinia zhar!"*

Far below me the world exploded into flames.

I was on my way; the flight of Vostok II had begun.

12. "I am Eagle . . . !"

A thundering waterfall of sound crashed into the spaceship's cabin. The clustered rocket motors of the great booster hurled sheets of flame across the launching pad, and through the sudden onslaught of vibration, I felt the first distinct movements upward from the earth. At first I felt little pressure, but the vibration was severer than I expected as Vostok shook from the energy release of the carrier rocket.

Then the vibration eased slightly; steadily it receded as a new force filled the cabin. The first touches of acceleration squeezed my body lightly. Then the embrace became stricter, more certain as acceleration forces increased, as the rocket gathered speed to itself. Soon I all but forgot the vibration as the gravity forces pushed my body down hard into the contour seat. As the earth fell away, a massive lead blanket squeezed oppressively about me; yet these forces were far less than I had endured in many hours of centrifuge training. The realization that the pressure came from my actual ascent toward space filled me with a sense of wonder and excitement. Even as the invisible acceleration pressed me downward I cried out involuntarily for the rocket to race faster, faster through the sky.

I pressed a button by my arm rest. An electric motor smoothly slid back the covering shield from a viewport near my head. I stared through in awe. Before my eyes the horizon expanded rapidly and the nearer surface of the earth was shrinking magically. I called to the command post: "Eagle[1] . . . all's well."

Through the continuous thunder I heard the radio crackle in my earphones and then the excited voice of the control center monitor coming through: "Eagle, Eagle. This is Spring One.[2] Command is following your flight . . . receiving your transmission . . . loud and clear . . . loud and clear . . . good luck . . . over."

"Spring One. Spring One. This is Eagle . . . Thank you . . . Thank you for your good wishes . . . Everything is going perfectly . . . Good health, comrades . . . good health . . . see you soon . . . see you soon . . . Eagle out . . . "

Entranced, I stared through the viewport. Strewn in morning mist, a mountain range appeared. Even as I looked down along the peaks, the scene continued to change. Ancient ridges like the wrinkled, weary faces of old men turned up to me, the mist adding touches of wispy beards and stray hairs. But the thundering rocket in its steady, accelerating ascent acted as a time machine. The beards of mist faded and the mountains grew younger before my eyes. The wrinkles dissolved into firm, hard lines and then smoothed out completely as the rocket booster steadily increased its velocity.

No longer did I rise vertically; the automatic pilot—a fabulous electronic brain—already commanded the motors to new positions. My angle to the earth no longer was vertical; the powerful booster bent in its flaming rush upward from the vertical, starting its lean toward the horizon—just as did the booster for the Vostok that preceded me. I glanced at the elapsed time, the accelerometer and gravity-force readings, cabin pressure, the altimeter . . . everything read perfectly, all lights in the green, everything moving exactly as scheduled. But I could not keep my eyes away from the porthole . . .

Almost as if I were looking through a motion picture camera

---

[1] Titov's call sign was *Oriel* (Eagle).
[2] Ground Command's call was *Zarya One* (Spring One).

that speeded up enormously, I watched the darkened side of mountains spring magically to brilliant life as my continuing ascent and increasing velocity scattered sunlight in all directions. I stared at plowed fields that shone with a deep blue-black color. As I rose toward the vacuum beyond earth I watched—steadily receding in size—lemon-colored fields of harvested wheat, forests of deep smoke-green color that seemed to float past the porthole, and clouds drifting above them. Amazingly sharp and clear in their definition, they were wind-filled sails hanging just above the surface.

The scene before my eyes was startling and incredibly beautiful, changing constantly. Deep blue shadows slid over the earth, contrasting starkly with the increasing brilliance of the sun. Here were majestic vistas far more imposing than the richest of wonders I had seen from my own jet fighter, soaring many miles above the earth in ghostlike flight.

Above all, the colors startled me. The earth flashed as a million-faceted gem, an extraordinary array of vivid hues that were strangely gentle in their play across the receding surface of the world. The light streaming into the cabin carried a strange shade as though it were filtered through stained glass.

It was a thousand times more beautiful than anything I could possibly have imagined.

And aside from the enormous weight of acceleration, flattening my body helplessly against the profile of the contour seat, I felt free of discomfort. In fact, I felt wonderful! There was not the slightest indication of dizziness from the original severe vibration. No nausea . . . or even the barest sign of any. I maintained a constant vigil over my reactions, trying to sense any change, no matter how slight, in sight, hearing or perception. But everything went perfectly, and I maintained a positive contact at all times with ground control.

The seconds became minutes; as time passed and the thundering roar continued, the scene through the porthole changed. No longer did I see sky, but a sharp line across the curving horizon, and absolute blackness beyond that. With Yuri's vivid descriptions to guide me, I knew what to look for; awed with the beauty of the sight, I had the advantage of studying it more carefully than had my friend, since I was anticipating the sight rather than being surprised by its appearance.

I could feel distinctly the moment when the great first-stage carrier rocket burned out. The tremendous gravity forces seemed to hesitate a moment, and then the next stage ignited with a dull crash far behind me. The Vostok leaped forward with ignition of the next stage, and the noise and vibration clearly decreased. Now I kept my eyes glued to the instruments, checking every detail, maintaining a running communications check with ground control. Radar tracking confirmed an excellent climb-out, a perfect programming of the rocket, excellent separation of the stages and perfect combustion in the upper stage—just as hoped for. I watched the hand of the chronometer as it swung closer and closer to the predicted moment of entering orbit.

The hand swung to its proper position. I felt a slight jolt as the last stage separated forcefully . . . instinctively I braced myself for the expected plunge into a condition of weightlessness.

There was nothing sudden in the transition. It came smoothly, spontaneously. I rejoiced in the sudden disappearance of the tremendous weight that had been pressing down so heavily upon my chest.

The weight vanished as quickly as Vostok separated from the booster . . . and I felt suddenly as though I were turning a somersault and then flying with my legs up!

For the life of me I could not determine where I was. I was completely confused, unable to define where was earth or the stars! It seemed as if the somersault had carried me completely around and that I was floating upside down, attached to nothing.

The instrument panel was bobbing around somewhere alongside me . . . everything whirled around in a strange fog that defied all my attempts to separate order from the sudden chaos. Something had gone suddenly and drastically wrong with the vestibular system of the inner ear—of my sense of balance. My sense of orientation vanished abruptly and completely.

Fortunately the sensation lasted only seconds. I forced myself to move my head sharply. All of a sudden things began to focus properly and everything again became clear. I studied the instrument panel. Magically it floated quietly back to its proper place. I blinked my eyes at the visual sensation . . . I turned to the porthole to locate the earth. The horizon cut across my field of vision exactly as it should; good. Then—the stars. The brilliant lights gleamed steadily at me.

I had mastered that mysterious sensation of plunging into weightlessness. The sudden tension of the moment disappeared quickly to be replaced with a sense of exhilaration, and I exulted in the feeling of release that comes with zero gravity.

Ground control obviously noted my temporary discomfort through the telemetered medical data from my body. A voice broke in sharply:

"Eagle . . . Eagle . . . This is Spring One. Report immediately on your condition. Over."

"Spring One . . . Spring One . . . This is Eagle. I feel magnificent . . . feel magnificent."

And I *did!*

I turned back to the instruments; a glance confirmed that the carrier rocket had injected Vostok II into orbit. Ground Control immediately came back on the radiophone with the full confirmation of the orbital data. My velocity at the moment was 17,750 miles per hour. The realization of the speed was almost staggering. There was absolutely no sensation of movement . . .

The additional data came in rapidly. My orbit was inclined sixty-four degrees fifty-six minutes to the equator. The computers flashed an orbital period for a complete revolution around the earth as 88.6 minutes. As Vostok II rushed around the planet, its low point of orbit, the perigee, came within one hundred and ten miles of the surface. Swinging around to the other side of the world, as computed by the great electronic brains, I would reach a height of just below one hundred and sixty miles.

Wonderful! The performance of the carrier rockets could not have been better—the orbit was more precise than that flown by Yuri on his mission. My spirits soared with the confirmation that I was truly committed to my flight through space, far above the world, independent of all weather, free of the atmosphere, well on my way to carrying out the first voyage of space ever made.

How different the earth looked now! There was the whole of the sphere, like something right out of a fairy tale. A planet enveloped in a blue coating and framed with a brilliant, radiant border. The sun burned fiercely through the viewports, shining with a terrible, intent brightness; it was unendurable for the human eye without protection.

I switched off the interior cabin lights to conserve battery power. Before long I had to bring them on again as the spaceship hurtled into the night side of the earth. Vostok II plunged with a rush into the inky blackness of the planet's shadow, and as my eyes quickly adapted to the change—before I turned the cabin illumination back on—I stared in wonder at huge stars that glittered like diamonds.

With a determined effort I turned my gaze from the magnificent display in the stellar heavens. There were specific tasks to fulfill. My program called for testing the manual control system, operating the different two-way radio communications facilities, monitoring the television cameras, checking the operation of the biotelemetering devices, and other assignments included in the flight program. For each of the scheduled seventeen circuits around the earth, I had a precise program to fulfill. Everything was worked out on a schedule—when to communicate with Ground Control, when to eat, exercise, drink, rest, sleep—even when to wake up.

Vostok II swung around for the first time from the earth's dark side when the Chief Constructor personally called via the radiophone. He gave to me the words I had been waiting for: "Eagle, Eagle. This is Spring One. This is Spring One. You may now take over manual control. You may now take over manual control. First, please check your cabin pressure. Repeat, first check your cabin pressure. Over . . . "

Everything moved perfectly . . . I had the miracle ship in my own hands just as I raced toward my first cosmic dawn. First there appeared a brilliant orange strata just above the horizon. Above this thin line all the colors of the rainbow began to appear, swelling in intensity until they loomed with a breathless clarity before my eyes. I felt as if I were studying the heavens through a great crystal prism. And then my orbital speed flung me from the absolutely black night into a bright sunlit day.

I stared down at the earth. I marveled at the clarity of the major rivers and mountains that appeared on the surface. It was possible even to distinguish cultivated land from the other areas that lay fallow without the mark of man upon them. The clouds were easily distinguishable from snow because of the bluish shadows that the drifting clouds cast beneath them. And as I raced past the dawn towards the sun, a lovely, powder-blue halo surrounded the planet.

"Eagle, Eagle . . . This is Spring One. Report how the manual control system is functioning. Report on the manual control system . . . Over." It was the Chief Constructor again.

"Spring One, Spring One. This is Eagle. Vostok responds to manual controls very well. The ship is very obedient. I consider the reaction speed sufficient for the first time . . . the angular speed presents no problems. Everything goes perfectly. I repeat . . . everything goes perfectly. Eagle over to Spring One."

At that moment I could imagine the look of triumph on the face of the Chief Constructor. A man in space . . . had controlled directly his own, marvelous creation. I wondered what that engineer would have given were it possible for him to personally be at these very same controls . . .

The rotating globe among the instruments indicated my position now as once again over the Soviet Union, approaching the same area where Yuri had landed, and where I myself was due to descend within less than twenty-four hours. The chronometer reading agreed that I was about to complete the first orbit—around the world in just under ninety minutes! It was a thrilling thought, especially with the realization that I would sweep in Vostok II around the earth once more, and still another fifteen times beyond that. Exactly at thirty-eight minutes after ten A.M., I radioed a message to the government of the U.S.S.R., the Central Committee of the Communist Party, and personally to Nikita Khrushchev:

"Attention, attention. Moscow, Kremlin. This is Eagle. Communist Party, Soviet government and, personally, to Nikita Sergeyevich Khrushchev: The flight of the Soviet Spaceship, Vostok II, is progressing successfully. All the equipment of the ship is functioning normally. I am feeling well. I ask you to convey warmest greetings to the whole Soviet people. Cosmonaut Titov . . ."

When again I looked through the viewport, I saw half the earth flooded with brilliant sunlight. Simultaneously within my gaze was the sight of stars that appeared huge and glittering, seeming to swarm so close to the spaceship that I felt I could reach out and touch them with my hands. The illusion was amazing.

In my first and second orbits I raced over the African continent. I found no difficulty in recognizing continents or large islands by their outlines. They look exactly as portrayed on global maps, but the effect of actually seeing the great land masses of the earth from space is a wonder that seems impossibly difficult to accept.

There are differences, of course; not only in their outlines but in their colors. It is astonishing how the earth stands out in so many vivid hues. Africa is distinctive in its markings; it is mainly a huge yellow mass with green jungle sprinkled across the surface, almost like a strangely mottled leopard skin. I recognized the Sahara Desert as a vast ocean of golden-brown sands revealing not a single sign of life. The golden color stopped abruptly at the edge of the

Mediterranean. That body of water by itself is one of the most spectacularly beautiful sights I have ever seen. It is dark blue along the edges of the land masses; as I rushed through space overhead it was painted a vivid ultramarine. Actually, it seemed to float slowly past the porthole, and was then swallowed up magically in the planet's haze. It was absolutely stunning in its beauty.

If space has its poetry, then it also has its prose. Aside from drinking in the marvels of the cosmic landscapes, my schedule demanded that I return frequently to the program of assignments. At all times that I orbited I transmitted data for the scientists on the ground. I accomplished this by either talking directly to a tracking station on the earth or, when I passed over long stretches of the planet without any receiving site below me, my words were taken down automatically on tape. Then, as I came within direct transmitting range of a station, the tape fed the recordings in fast bursts of sound to the station, later to be replayed at the proper speed.

Constantly I recorded information on the reading of my instuments; on the temperature, pressure and humidity of the cabin; how all equipment functioned; how I felt personally during the mission. The sensors taped to my body fed a constant stream of vital medical data either through direct transmission, or also into the tapes. They recorded such things as the electric potentials and the mechanical activity of my heart, the frequency and depth of respiration, my temperature, and my blood circulation. If I erred at any time in my reports of my own physical condition, the technicians on the ground could immediately notice the discrepancy of the voice reports against the information shown in the data telemetered from the body sensors.

Actually, the doctors on earth saw a far more accurate presentation of my body functions than I could give them in words. Not only could they read the data presented before them electronically —as well as judging me objectively—but they had displayed before them at almost all times television pictures of me in the spaceship. They added to their medical data sometimes by direct queries on different points. During the third orbit, for example, I received this call:

"Eagle, Eagle . . . This is Spring One. Please report on your reactions to weightlessness. Does your belt apply any pressure to either your left or right side? Repeat—does your belt apply any body pressure to your left or right side? Over."

"Spring One, Spring One. This is Eagle. The belt has not applied any unexpected body pressures anywhere. Repeat—I have no difficulties with the belt of any kind. I am very comfortable. My condition is excellent. I feel fine . . . feel fine. Over."

Aside from these direct radiophone communications my schedule demanded that I transmit a position report by shortwave radio twice every hour, regardless of my position around the world.

Vostok II contained three radio-telephone systems. A Very High Frequency (VHF) system worked with marvelous clarity but was effective for communications to a range of only a thousand miles or so. Its greatest asset was its freedom from any electronic disturbances from the ionosphere, permitting the best reception. I used the VHF system each time I passed over the Soviet Union, transmitting and receiving with the nearest ground control center or tracking station.

The other two radios were High Frequency (HF) systems which I could use simultaneously to transmit and receive messages at any time and over any distance. The quality was not of the best, but the HF systems served their purpose perfectly well.

Apart from my own voice messages and the medical and television transmissions, Vostok II was alive with a battery of transmitters. Automatic equipment steadily radioed to earth a stream of information on external temperatures of the spaceship, cosmic radiation levels, meteoric impacts against the metal skin, and similar data.

During the space flight I was able to speak with many of my closest friends and associates, including the Chief Constructor, Cosmonaut 3, Dr. Anatolyevitch, and with other scientists and engineers. I regretted not being able to communicate directly with the scientist who had plotted the infinitely complicated orbital calculations. Unfortunately, he had left the main Control Center for a computer installation, where he did not have the means to establish direct voice contact with me as the spaceship flashed overhead.

" . . . Eagle . . . Eagle. This is Spring One. This is Spring One. Request that you concentrate for a while on general impressions of the flight. Repeat—you are requested to concentrate on the general impressions of the flight. How does the earth appear to you? What can you see of the earth through your viewing ports? Over."

"Spring One. Spring One. This is Eagle. Understand you. Understand your request . . . Everything is fine. The earth seems to be above me. Repeat—the earth seems to be above me. This feeling is very strong when the earth disappears from my direct vision. This is most pronounced when I view the earth from the upper viewing port . . . then the earth looks like part of an enormous globe that is suspended in space. When the earth is in shadow . . . I can see a brilliant, thin crescent line. The visual impression is amazing. At the moment a vast space that I am observing is mostly covered with clouds . . . the sun's reflection is very bright. This is Eagle . . . Over."

In this manner went my communications with earth, transmitting each time as I whirled around the planet more and more information of space, of the view of the world, of my own feelings, the performance of my equipment. Every minute of the mission contributed vital data to our scientists; every transmission added to the solid foundation of the science of cosmic flight. It is the same in any endeavor of this nature, but I felt a deep and wonderful elation at the realization that *my* flight—at this very moment—had already provided more invaluable data to our scientists than all the robot and manned flights into space ever made. It is a moving thing to realize you are standing at the crossroads of the future, to know that by your own doing you will affect the path that man will select for his travels.

Even the most serious of moments, however, must yield to the personality of the people involved. As I orbited, I kept a promise to one of the cosmonauts—the same pilot who had astounded us so with his intent painting in the Chamber of Silence (and that seemed so incredibly long ago as I thought of it!).

"Bring us back some cosmic colors, Gera," was his request, and now I did my best to comply. Certainly the colors were all about me; the most intense and incredible colors that any man had ever seen, a riot of hues that blended and shifted before my eyes, a rush of dawns and sunsets, colors truly of the earth . . . but to be seen only from the far distances of space itself.

I pointed the Konvass camera at the horizon, holding it as close as possible to the viewport. The camera was nothing more than a standard model in fairly wide use, and I am no expert. But luck was with me, and as it turned out we had some stunning photographs to show of the horizon and the edge of the sea of space—in brilliant color.

Throughout the mission the atmosphere in the cabin remained exactly as we had planned. The air regeneration equipment, located behind the pilot's compartment, maintained an exact "microclimate." The equipment absorbed the carbon dioxide and water vapor that were given off by my respiratory processes, and a constant flow of oxygen and other gases flowed through the cabin. At all times, sensitive counters checked the level of the carbon dioxide and oxygen, as well as the cabin humidity. Any deviation from the tolerances which were programmed was noted by electronic "watchdogs;" these in turn flashed signals to an automatic controller that adjusted immediately the gaseous content and percentages in the cabin.

I could set the temperature for any level between fifty degrees and seventy-seven degrees Fahrenheit, and the automatic control system would maintain that temperature exactly at the desired level.

The entire system performed flawlessly. I hurtled through space for the entire mission with a cabin atmospheric pressure slightly above that of sea level. The oxygen content was maintained at exactly 24.33 percent of the cabin pressure. Carbon dioxide levels were never a problem, since they averaged out at only 0.4 percent for the flight. The relative humidity in the cabin fluctuated between seventy and seventy-five percent.

I orbited the earth in the equivalent of a small planet with superb weather conditions.

There was always the danger, of course, that something would go wrong with the system—by virtue of the fact that *any* machinery or equipment can fail. The air regeneration system itself might develop some difficulties. Even if everything worked perfectly, there was always the danger that a small meteor might puncture the tough shell of the spaceship, causing a sudden and dangerous explosive loss of pressure. If any of these possibilities came to pass, the glass visor of my helmet would slam shut automatically. A standby cabin system for air flow and pressure would kick into action, feeding me the required atmospheric conditions through the sealed spacesuit itself. Fortunately none of these things happened, and not once during the entire mission did Vostok's superb equipment so much as falter.

My third turn around the earth brought me over the entire length of the Pacific Ocean—a breathless sweep from Vladivostok in the northwest down the vast expanse of ocean, around the bottom of Cape Horn in the southeast and then over the full length of the Atlantic. My course would skirt the east coast of South America and then the west coast of Africa, swinging from Cape Horn to Gibraltar. It was a marvelous travel itinerary, but even as I was flung by the Vostok's orbital speed around an entire planet, my duties continued. On this orbit I was to eat my first food in space, but I cannot speak well for the menu.

It was without enthusiasm that I reached for the food containers. At no time have I ever been one to enjoy food for the sake of special dishes. Personally, I would have preferred not to bother with the food, but this was an essential part of the program for weightless condition tests.

The beige-colored metal food container had several slots for the tubes, with a switch at the side for heating the tubes before I opened them. I picked out a bronze tube—which bore the name Mikoyan Food Plant, Moscow, on its side—about the size of a large tube of toothpaste. The identification tab said that the tube contained four ounces of soup puree.

I unscrewed the tab, holding it tightly between my fingers so that it would not drift away across the cabin. Then I placed the end of the tube in my mouth and squeezed gently—and I could not rid myself of the sensation that I was about to squeeze a whole tube of toothpaste into my mouth.

But the taste of the soup puree was unmistakable. When the tube was empty I screwed the cap back on, shoved the flattened tube into the disposal container, and selected a tube of meat and liver paste. With this I drew out several miniature rolls of concentrated bread. These were only about one inch in diameter, allowing the eater to place the whole lot in his mouth at once. Otherwise, Vostok II's tidiness would have been upset by dozens of crumbs floating about gently in the cabin—with no place to fall under the zero gravity.

Next, I washed down my lunch with a tube of red currant juice. My success in eating with neatness in weightlessness vanished when I drank the juice. Some of the liquid leaked from the tube and instinctively I reached out to brush the spacesuit. But nothing touched the suit . . . the drops of juice hung like berries before my face, and then floated around in the air with a slight quivering motion, almost as if they were small soap bubbles. I reached out gently and scooped them into my mouth—marvelous!

I could have finished lunch with coffee and cream, or chocolate, also contained in tubes. I preferred water; from a rubber-capped pipe that led down into a triangular-shaped white tank I sucked water into my mouth. Satisfied that this worked well, I popped some vitamin pills in my mouth and washed them down with some more water. There were no problems at any time from eating while under conditions of weightlessness.

Although my attitude toward lunch had been indifferent, I felt definitely better after eating. Now my schedule called for a period of rest, but I simply felt too good to lie back without anything to do.

The camera was floating in mid-air near me and I leaned over to snatch it with my hand. As I did so the log book drifted upward from my knees and began to drift away from me. The opportunity was too good to miss; I shot some pictures of the log book as it hung magically in front of me. Then I held the camera in front of me, adjusted the lens for portrait distance, and took pictures of myself. I was unable to resist winking at the camera as I clicked the release.

The spaceship raced again toward the shadow of the earth; as the great curving line of blackness ridged with brilliant red and orange light hurtled toward Vostok, I shot more film through the viewport. Once into the almost total darkness, I pointed the camera upward at the moon and the stars.

The visual perspective at such moments was completely unexpected. To me it appeared as if the spaceship were not moving, as though I were suspended in space by some invisible force. The impression was overwhelming that I had no motion whatsoever—and that it was the crescent moon that flung itself with great speed past the viewport. I was surprised, and a bit disappointed, that the moon did not differ greatly from our view of it from this world as we see it standing on the earth.

Each time Vostok made the transition from darkness to the

illuminated side of the earth, I found it impossible to tear my eyes from the viewport. Before the spaceship fled out of the earth's shadow, the movement of twilight across the planet's surface became one of the most inspiring sights I have ever seen. The edge of light and darkness was amazingly distinct.

I stared at one side of the huge globe, dazzling in the light of the sun, while simultaneously I could see the other side shrouded in absolute blackness. Separating the two areas was a fleeting, gray belt of twilight with small clouds, sprayed to a shell-pink by the setting sun.

Every time I looked at earth, every time I stared down at the world of men, I saw sights not merely unusual, but vibrant with color and that constant sense of incredulity.

No matter what the official commissions and the scientists of different nations may say to support their extensive projects to explore space, I know that the sea of space through which our world swims awaits not only the scientists and the technicians for testing and analyzing, but also the poets, the artists, and the composers.

It is a sight to stir a man deeply in a manner he can never possibly forget. The sight of a man's planet below him in all its beauty burns itself forever into his mind.

Nothing impresses man with the awesome power that hurls him into the void beyond our atmosphere than a single glance which, by itself, reduces the individual creations of nature to miniature gems. At one point in orbit the dazzling white peaks of the Himalayas and the Tien Shan Mountains lay squarely across my path of flight. From my boyhood I knew the stories of these mountains well, of their grandeur and their stupendous size.

Now, looking down from my spaceship, they appeared as tiny white mounds separated by deep blue lines—the great valleys of the highest mountains on earth. I might have been looking down through a microscope.

Each of the oceans and the seas, as the continents, reveal themselves with particular coloration and geographical characteristics. The very first sweeps around the planet brought me over the Pacific and the Atlantic oceans. Staring down with the naked eye, from my height they appeared to be absolutely calm. But under the optical horizon scanners that magnified my view three and five times, I could actually distinguish the endless swells as they heaved their way across the Pacific, and cut even wider swaths as I watched over the surface of the Atlantic. The Indian Ocean spread brilliantly in a rich indigo blue . . . the Gulf of Mexico lay across the world as a startling salad-green color . . . but the Mediterranean glistened like a vast sea of shining emeralds.

Each hour in space seemed to bring with it a sight more beautiful than the wonders I had just passed. On my third turn about the earth, as I swung around the planet's darkened side, a shimmering light in the absolute blackness drew my attention. The light became ever more beautiful as I rushed closer and closer at nearly eighteen thousand miles per hour. Quickly I checked the cross-sights of the navigation globe; the lights came from the city of Rio de Janeiro.

If those people knew the incredible beauty they present to a traveler of space! The shimmering light became a wonderfully rich gold dust, sparkling and gleaming against a backdrop of velvet blackness. Then, as I passed almost over the city, I traced a network of finely illuminated lines—the lighted highways of the city flowing in toward a central glow of orange.

My next global circuit in the earth's night side sent Vostok plunging down a line through the center of Latin America from south to north. . . . The fifth turn brought me over Edinburgh, then a rush across Siberia and China, a hurtling swing over the center of Australia and an eager look forward once again to see South America, this time directly over the city of Lima, Peru.

It was marvelous to ghost through space at three hundred miles every minute, and simply by dialing the ordinary radio receiver to hear the voices of men talking in many different languages. Passing over Russia I heard the first announcement from Radio Moscow of the flight of Vostok II and learned—from a height above my country of nearly seven hundred thousand feet—that I had been promoted in the Air Force to major's rank. I welcomed the news, and knew even as Radio Moscow's broadcast went out, that the cosmonauts' wives would be heaping their congratulations upon Tamara.

Tamara . . . . I wonder what she thought as she discovered that I was even at that moment rushing through the vacuum of space.

From every continent on the earth I heard references to my flight as I passed over the different nations of the world. Although I could not understand the different languages, I could readily distinguish Vostok and Khrushchev and, of course, my own name. At one point, listening to a broadcast in Russian from one of the European nations, I burst out with a roar of laughter. As I passed over the country I heard the announcer denying flatly that any Russian spaceship had been launched, and that Cosmonaut Titov didn't even exist. It was a wonderful moment.

On the sixth orbit over the Soviet Union, Ground Control relayed a message from Yuri. I shouted with joy as I learned that he was flying back to Russia to be with me.

Each time Vostok II whirled around the earth I continued marking off the different assignments as listed on my work schedule. One such task involved physical exercise; our doctors were keenly interested on what physical exertion under zero-gravity might do to the body. I was to exercise my abdominal muscles by trying as hard as I could to pull myself away from the belts that strapped me in across the waist. Other exercises carefully worked out by the doctors to tone up different muscles, joints and limbs, considered the condition of weightlessness and my confinement to the pilot's contour seat. I felt definitely better after they were completed, and the doctors reported no problems from the exercises.

The ship's log carried a separate page for each of the expected seventeen orbits, with a requirement that I write notes on each page through the mission. My pencil was secured with a thin line to the log; I kept the book on my knees, holding it pressed firmly down with one hand while I wrote. If I removed my hand for so much as an instant, the log started to drift away from me. In order to get all my notes down I found it necessary to write as quickly as possible—both of the technical accounting of the flight and my own swiftly-changing impressions of what I could see through the viewports.

Every stroke of the pencil was a new experiment. I knew that after the flight specialists and doctors would examine with microscopic detail every stroke, line, dot and comma to study what effect weightlessness had on my handwriting, which in itself is an unusually good exercise in coordination. But when I looked at the uneven scrawls that formed most of the log-book entries, I had to smile. It was exactly the same uneven, awkward penmanship for which my wife and friends reproached me under perfectly normal conditions of gravity. In order to spare the scientists much time and effort—including perhaps a whole new theory on coordination under weightlessness!—I emphasized in the log that my writing, odd as it might seem to them, was no worse than it had always been.

On my sixth orbit I received confirmation of the schedule to return the attitude of the spaceship to manual control. The first time I manipulated the reaction controls I moved slowly and cautiously. Now I enjoyed much more confidence in the system and my own abilities. I flicked the switch on the dashboard at my left to activate the manual system.

I closed my right hand smoothly and surely around the black handle. Immediately a thrill shot through me! What a tremendous feeling to manipulate with just my hand the mass of a spaceship plunging through vacuum at nearly eighteen thousand miles per hour! No matter what impressions I had before, no matter what my previous thoughts, the sensation came to me as fully as if this were the first time I had ever touched that black handle.

In the palm of my right hand was the precision control for the mightiest piece of equipment in which man has ever flown, a vessel of space that by virtue of its proven performance stands out years ahead of anything even distantly comparable. The control handle obeyed the flexing of my wrist muscles, the pressure of my fingers, like a well-trained animal.

Racing through space at five miles a second, Vostok II eased her bulk around with excellent precision and response. Left and right, up and down, rolling around her axis, swinging through turns—anything I transmitted to the spaceship through no more than the subtle manipuation of the handle brought an instant and completely obedient reaction.

I rejoiced in the power that moved beneath me. All I need do was to select any spot in the world that appeared within the hair-thin cross sight on the navigation globe, and there I could descend from space for a landing. No more than the flick of another switch and the globe would rotate swiftly to display to me the actual landing area.

The schedule called for only twenty minutes of manual flight control at this time; regretfully I passed the spaceship's stabilization system back to her automatic pilot.

The hours passed quickly; before I realized how much time had fled, the schedule called for dinner. I thought of home and my wife. Sometimes Tamara had almost to force me to eat. Here, in space, I had no wife to fret over my meals, no one to stand by impatiently until I bolted my food. No wife, no instructor—except a printed line on my flight instructions. And that was stricter by far than even Tamara when her temper flared!

There could be no deviation from the planned schedule. Not a single iota of change. This was a matter of the severest training and discipline. Everything for this flight had been carefully planned for years in order that our scientists might realize the maximum possible benefit from every moment. That was the policy of our space program. Do not waste time and effort by repeating experiments; conduct each one in the most thorough and meticulous fashion. Quite a speech for myself simply to accept the idea of eating again, but as before I did not look forward eagerly to food. Quickly I squeezed my tubes of meat paste and currant juice and bolted down the meal.

The chronometer hand turned . . . the earth ground slowly around on its axis . . . and in my time machine I flashed through the dawns and twilights. Each time I swung through the belt of transition I regained that sense of sudden wonder at actually hurtling through a full day and night in less than one and a half hours. Each time I stared in awe again, never for an instant tiring of the miraculous sight of which writers and poets had dreamed for so many years . . . .

I could not evade the sensation of strangeness I felt from seeing the absolute black dome of space always above me, and the rich blue of the terrestrial sky below, with Vostok sailing serenely in between the two—an amazing separation of vacuum and atmosphere, of space and a world of men.

Then something new—something odd—caught my eye. I stared through the viewport; if I could believe what I saw, then I had acquired a *second* sky.

After making six orbits of the planet, the view of space no longer seemed to contain the intense blackness I noted so clearly during my initial hours in space. No longer could I accurately describe space as a "black void."

Nor did the earth now disappear completely from view when my spaceship fell with its tremendous speed into the planet's shadow. Without any question of what I saw I could distinguish through the blackness of night the shape of the earth below, and its scattered blankets of clouds.

What caused this sudden night visibility I do not know. Perhaps the thin crescent moon passed on enough of the sun's reflected light to increase the night shine of the earth. It might even be light reflected from the atmosphere itself, acting in some fashion as a prism. It might be a combination of both. Whatever the cause for the unexpected change in night-side illumination, it would provide much food for thought for our astronomers and scientists.

The birth of each new day came smoothly and with no diminishing of beauty. Each time I passed around the earth, I saw a different scene below me of continental areas, bodies of water, and islands. Never could I tire of watching those fabulous dawns of space . . . the almost imperceptible transition of rich color, the first hues of the onrushing sun bathing gently the interior of the spaceship cabin.

So quiet, so soft were the beginnings of each transition that the sudden change to an almost explosive change in light and color took my breath away. The sun hurtled from behind the great rounded flanks of the earth, within a minute or two blazing in the skies against a backdrop of black, bringing a rich light swimming all about me in Vostok.

Except when the rapid passage about the earth of the spaceship brought the sun to shine directly into the viewport. At such moments, that distant star became savage in its intensity, unbearable to the eyes. It was as though I stared directly into a thousand arc lamps, each more painfully bright than the other. On such occasions—as experience from the first encounter with the naked sun taught me—I quickly flicked a switch with my finger. Electric motors whined softly and an opaque shield slid at once over the viewport.

During daylight the horizon assumed a sharp white color, covered everywhere with its characteristic blue halo. Each time I studied the curving horizon I gained once again a feeling of tremendous height. No; *height* is a poor phrase in this instance. It would be more accurate to say a sensation of distance, of *perspective*. You can never shake off the impact of sensing the *roundness* of man's home planet.

While the dawns progressed from a long moment of subtlety to an explosive arrival of dazzling brilliance, entering the cosmic night was an unhurried process to delight the eyes and souls of poets. Marching across the planet in a circlet of deep red-orange, the vivid sunset yielded unwillingly to the dark shrouds that advanced to envelop the light of day. Fiery colors blazed along the tidal wave of demarcation, flashing colors to the horizon where the blue halo increased its richness of hues until by some magic of transformation night reigned supreme.

Only forty-five minutes between each sunset and each dawn, between dawn and sunset, and each of these sights producing ever new, always profoundly moving impressions. Six complete days and nights within little more than an ordinary eight-hour working day!

Small wonder that I felt elation as I had never before known in my life . . . the miracles of space before my eyes to drink in hour after hour; the realization of the most fantastic dream that men have ever dared to nourish in their minds . . . the superb performance of all my equipment in an environment so hostile as to defy a true impression. And all this, this . . . incredible sweep, was mine; to see and sense and wonder, and later to carry it back to the planet with me. I felt no later reflection or regret once when, feeling as I did, I replied to a call from earth with the cry: "I am Eagle! I am Eagle!"

For a long moment there was silence from the ground station; that was all as the normal transmissions between earth and space continued. But there was no doubt, as I was to learn later, that my elation was known . . . and that it found a compassionate understanding on the planet that rolled far beneath me.

And yet, as the movement of the chronometer needle erased the seconds and swept the minutes into hours, I began finally to sense a definite element of fatigue. The sheer intensity of everything happening began to exact its toll. The accumulation of more than nine hours of sustained, uninterrupted weightlessness—preceded by the conscious *and* subconscious knowledge that I was moving through an area so raw and virgin that medical science could provide assistance only with educated guesses—all this finally produced its reaction.

It would be an error to attempt to specify with exactness a physiological reaction of the flight that occurred next; because we are so much in need of greater understanding of man remaining under zero gravity, many explanations are sorely in need. But there is no question that—whether objective or subjective—the sustained weightlessness affected me in a manner unanticipated.

The correct orientation and the coordination of movements of a man in space rely heavily upon the proper functioning of three body systems. These include the vestibular apparatus; eyesight for visual references; and the receptory apparatus of the body such as the skin, muscles, tendons, joints and the connecting tissues. My problem was that I began suddenly to experience difficulties with one of these key elements—the vestibulary apparatus.

This represents a very intricate play of biological mechanics in which a major role is played by the *otoliths*. These are small crystals of calcium carbonate and phosphate, imbedded in a jelly-like mass which in turn is housed in a sac of fluid within the inner ear. It is a neatly packed and finely adjusted biological instrument.

Under ordinary conditions on the surface of the earth, the otoliths change position whenever the position of the head changes; the sensation of change is transmitted instantly along a nerve to the individual's central nervous system. Upon "receipt" of this message the nervous system flashes instructions to the appropriate muscles so that the body may maintain its proper sense of balance when in motion, *or its position in relation to gravity on the earth's surface*.

The human race has evolved under the conditions particular to the surface of our planet. One of those conditions, known identically throughout the entire existence of man, has been a steady force of gravity. The system of balance for the brain, the nervous system, and the body thus is a product of evolution under these specified conditions.

But while I orbited the earth in Vostok II, I had eliminated these conditions for all my orbital time. As a satellite of the earth, my spaceship was actually *falling* around the planet. A man *feels* gravity on earth because the ground beneath his feet provides him with a feeling or a sense of *support*. In space, without an atmosphere to impede the rush of the spacecraft as it fell about the planet in its orbit, there was no support either for Vostok II or for myself. Nothing impeded the movement of my spaceship—nothing interfered with its fall. Deprived of support such as a man feels on earth, or even in an airplane cruising above the earth, we were deprived of the sense of gravity.

Thus I existed in a condition of zero gravity, or no-weight. Under this condition, the body's otoliths cannot function properly. Their system of informing the brain of changes of pressure in relationship to the familiar downward force of gravity vanishes. There is no sense of balance in the accepted sense of the word for a man on earth.

Under certain conditions the loss of the function provided by the otoliths "scrambles" the sense of balance. This is what affected me so starkly during those first several seconds when the spaceship separated from the carrier rocket and entered orbit; i.e., a condition of zero gravity. Fortunately, I was able quickly to overcome the loss of balance and regain my bearings.

But now, after more than nine hours of continuous exposure to weightlessness, I was once again having a difficult time in maintaining a precise sense of balance. This became unquestionable to me when I began to experience moments of dizziness, and then, nausea. The moments caused additional distress when they repeated at more frequent intervals, until the sensations were fixed.

To offset the lack of function of the otoliths, I made every effort to move my head as little as possible. Unfortunately, the fatigue of the nine hours in flight cost me in mental acuity. I found that unexpectedly I *was* moving my head—until a wave of nausea sharply reminded me of what I was doing.

I noticed that when I observed something in rapid movement— a dial or a meter in the cabin, for example—the same dizziness and nausea increased. Despite the discomfort accompanying these symptoms, I carefully noted them in my log book and informed Ground Control of the problem.

Not at all unwelcome to me was the next required step on the flight schedule—sleep. During my seventh orbit I flashed over Moscow at 6:15 P.M. While daylight showed clearly in the city, I prepared for sleep. Everything in the spaceship cabin was perfect; all systems operated exactly as planned.

It is important to stress that while I suffered a definite discomfort from the nausea and the dizziness, these reactions at no time interfered with the performance of my duties as they were scheduled.

I arranged with Ground Control to discontinue all radio transmissions, although the receivers in both Vostok II and all ground stations would remain open in event of anything unexpected.

I released special belts from the side of the pilot's seat that had been installed for the sleep period, and strapped my body to the seat. Then I adjusted the contour seat to the bed position.

My last thoughts were comforting. Vostok II plunged around the world in an orbit that could keep the spaceship aloft for many days, perhaps weeks. An army of small robot mechanisms silently whirred and hummed as they transmitted back to earth a constant stream of data on both my own body functions and those of the spaceship. The television cameras maintained a constant surveillance of my face and body.

And down below . . . far below on earth, Dr. Yevgenyi Anatolyevich kept an electronic finger on my pulse.

I went to sleep.

13. Return to Earth

I blinked my eyes. The soft lights of the spaceship cabin bathed the instrument panel. For a moment I stayed quiet; deliberately I did not move.

Something was wrong.

Immediately I sensed this; I had awakened much earlier than my plans called for. I turned my eyes to the orbit counter; Vostok hurtled effortlessly through space on her eighth swing about the planet.

It *was* too early. I turned my eyes to look forward, and at the same moment I knew why a sixth sense had aroused me from sleep.

My arms dangled weightlessly . . . my hands floated in mid-air, drifting ever so slightly with the forced draft in the cabin. The sight was incredible.

I pulled my arms down and folded them across my chest. Everything was fine—until I relaxed.

My arms floated away from me again as quickly as the conscious pressure of my muscles relaxed and I passed into sleep. Two or three attempts at sleep in this manner proved fruitless.

Finally I tucked my arms beneath a belt. Then I tried gently to lift them up. Good! They remained where they were. In seconds I was again sound asleep.

Once you've got your arms and legs arranged properly, space sleeping is fine. There's no need to turn over from time to time as a man normally does in his own bed. Because of the condition of weightlessness there's no pressure on the body; nothing goes numb. It's marvelous; the body is extraordinarily light and buoyant.

Considering the manner in which I usually sleep on the earth, however, my first slumber in the cosmos was not all that it should have been. I awoke this first time as described, but something must have tugged annoyingly at my mind when I dozed off again. I woke up twice more during the sleep period—something in a comparable period of time I never do normally. The second awakening came during the tenth orbit; the third during the eleventh orbit. After that I slept like a baby.

When I opened my eyes again and saw the time, my first thoughts were of trouble. Not with the spaceship, but with Ground Control. It was 2:37 A.M. Moscow Time, and I was a full thirty minutes behind schedule because of oversleeping. But Ground Control never mentioned my laxity, even though it put the program behind the scheduled events, and I had to readjust my own activities in the spaceship. I should have awakened over the equator, but it was actually somewhere going down the Pacific, between Australia and the United States.

The moment I saw the chronometer I quickly scanned the instruments; everything checked out normally. Then one of the doctor's voices from Ground Central came over the radio, asking me how I felt. I even forgot the call letters, and simply said, "Fine. . . ." Immediately after this I called out the instrument readings as I had been doing.

But the doctor's query reminded me that I was late in performing my physical exercises. I still was required to do the "morning calisthentics" as part of the schedule of events, even if I was in space. I stretched my legs, flexed and tensed my muscles, moved my arms up and bent them rapidly, clenched and unclenched my fists, and went through as many other exercises as a man can do while he's strapped down to a spaceship's contour seat under zero gravity.

After this I felt wonderful. Most of the nausea and dizziness I'd known so strongly before falling asleep were gone. They had not left entirely, but the intensity of the feeling was diminished greatly.

In terms of the tremendous excitement I had known up to this part of the mission, the remaining orbits might accurately be described as routine. I carried out all scheduled assignments, but the growing air of repetition for this work made me regard it as akin to the work a pilot does on an extended cross-country flight. It is a matter of routine, the pilot knows what to expect and while every move he makes is an essential one, his actions are more a matter of trained reflex than something he does with a conscious appreciation of his activities.

At no time did I lose my sense of wonder at the stark beauty that paraded before me in space, accelerated by the time factor of Vostok II's tremendous velocity around the planet. But this time, instead of the breathless excitement that had kept me to an acute sense of observation before I slept, I made more leisurely visual observations. Now there was the opportunity to "sit back and take a second look." I did exactly that.

As I came around the planet for the seventeenth orbit, the feeling of routine vanished abruptly. From the moment the spaceship whipped around the globe into the seventeenth orbit, things became *much* livelier. Now there was exacting, critical work to do . . . preparing myself for the precarious plunge back into the atmosphere of the earth, with all the speed of a meteor.

My final dawn—the seventeenth in space—approached me with a beauty unlike all the others I had seen in the last day. The first light of dawn illuminated with the faintest touch the distant sweeping curve of the earth. Then into view came the vivid crescent line, rainbow-hued, still impossible to believe in its stunning sight. Beyond, there lay a velvet blackness, a backdrop of absolutely black heavens framing the rainbow dawn, the whole of the mantle pierced by brilliant pinpoints of stars. I am at a loss to capture the true immensity of this scene, but its grandeur struck me with almost a physical force, and completely entranced me.

Through the wonder I felt there intruded the very grim facts of life. Beautiful as was this seventeenth dawn, it was also dangerous.

This was to be the moment of truth for the flight of Vostok II. And despite all the confidence that one has, despite all the assurances and the proven reliability, this is the moment that the man in space fears. Except for the extremely remote possibility of dual failures of the spaceship cabin and the pressure-suit system in space, I was completely *safe*. But now I was to leave the environment where everything is precise and mathematical, to plunge back into the swirling blanket that protects our planet.

The atmosphere of earth could not distinguish between a manned spaceship and a meteor plunging from vacuum. It would resist the passage of both by virtue of friction of those objects through that atmosphere. That friction may well come to be known among space-flight circles as the "baptism of fire" before earth once again accepts its own.

Invisible commands from the tracking stations and ships on the planet's surface had already taken their effect within Vostok. The instruments displayed visually the motions already begun by the robot brain to establish the exact attitude of the spaceship along its orbital path. Everything must be precise, with no margin for error allowed.

I received verification from a tracking ship of the flight mechanics and data, and made a hair-trigger adjustment of one control knob. Although my body could not yet sense anything different about the orbital flight, psychologically I seemed to gain the impression of my tremendous speed as the moment for firing the retro-rockets approached.

I braced myself in the seat, already angled properly to enable me best to resist the forces of deceleration that would soon strike. Once again time hung on the sweeping motion of that hand on the chronometer dial.

The fire in front of Vostok II began. An automatic switch triggered precisely on schedule. Lances of fire stabbed the vacuum before my hurtling spaceship.

Weightlessness began to melt from me. As the sensation of floating fell away, simultaneously the noise and the vibration of the rockets increased. Then the retros were at maximum boost.

With full deceleration under way the braking impact hit me with all the force of a pile driver. Deceleration ground me into the seat as Vostok II abandoned space for the upper edges of the atmosphere. The blazing exhausts of the retros mingled with the brilliant orange flames of the spaceship's outer hull as the heat shield in front of Vostok II took the brunt of the intense friction.

Pinned to my seat, I gasped for breath under the tremendous pressure to which re-entry now subjected me. But after several seconds I knew this would be no worse than I had known many times on the centrifuges in my training, and Yuri had endured the same forces before me.

I moved my head slightly to look through the viewport. It was like staring into the blazing maw of an erupting volcano. Flames streaked past the windows in a blur of white-hot light, the twin stabs of retro-fire mingling with the blazing gases that surrounded Vostok II in their fiery cocoon. And yet the sensation of heat was entirely visual; the temperatures within the spaceship remained as before, although I knew that the refrigeration system at this moment was at maximum capacity.

As the spaceship hurtled back toward earth in a long, curving line of deceleration fire, I recalled what Yuri had said to me of this moment in his own descent: ". . . the overloads were tremendous, but just to get back to earth again I could have supported a whole mountain on my shoulders! I don't know whether or not they heard me on the ground, but I was shouting like a drunk, again and again—'I'll be home! I'll be home!' "

Now I knew the intense feelings that ran beneath those simple words! Without warning the yearning for earth, for home, strikes hard. The time I had just spent beyond the world showed me clearly enough that there will be for men in space a monotony and a loneliness; but these are negative emotions and they cannot possibly compare with the exultation of anticipating the feel of solid earth beneath your feet—and the desire to see the heavens where they have always been. *Up. Above* me!

I felt the slightest lessening of the deceleration forces, and a glance at the instruments confirmed that the worst was behind me. The retro-rockets were almost through their firing cycle. For several minutes I had been out of radio contact with the earth as a shell of ionized gases blazed around the spaceship, acting as a communications shield. But with the friction forces of re-entry almost gone, I rejoiced to hear a friendly voice coming through the earphones again, calling out an altitude reading for me to check against my own instruments.

The doctors didn't even ask me to report on my condition; with the resumption of communications they could see for themselves the reports on the medical monitoring panel. To say nothing of the grin that crossed my face as they saw the scene on their television monitors. A wonderful thing—having the doctors able to *watch* me directly with their own eyes while I was in space through the flight!

No longer did I feel the vibration of the motors and the minor oscillations of the re-entry forces that crashed against the spaceship; gone, too, was the powerful roar of the rockets and the re-entry maneuver as Vostok II slammed back into the atmosphere. The refrigeration plant had added its own racket to the din as it spun at full speed to compensate for the thousands of degrees that blazed along the external hull of the spaceship. All this was behind me. . . .

Vostok II was once again within the comforting lower atmosphere of the planet; except for the seared surfaces where the heat had been greatest along the hull, the spaceship came through unscathed. But there was still work to be done, still specific procedures to follow. Yuri had returned to the earth's surface within his spaceship, but my own descent would be different.

Vostok II fell like a stone through the air, stabilized in an arrow-like drop toward the earth. I activated several switches and controls, gripped the contour seat carefully, and glued my eyes on the chronometer. The sweep hand came around, moving steadily closer to the moment when explosive charges would go off, and I would be hurled with the seat away from the falling spaceship. Ten—then only three more seconds to go. A red light flashed on the indicator panel. . . .

Thunder crashed into my ears at the same instant I felt a tremendous force beneath me. The ejection shell exploded exactly on schedule, and in a blur I saw daylight flash before my eyes as the entire seat burst away from the spaceship. For the first time in more than twenty-five hours, like a prisoner released from a cell, the entire sky presented itself in one swift glance to me. The horizon tilted sharply, clouds came into my line of sight, and then the earth rolled cleanly before me again.

I caught a glimpse of the spaceship falling rapidly away beneath me; abruptly it disappeared within a small cloud. The next moment the separation device pushed my body away from the seat and my own parachute spilled into the air, opening with a wonderful, muffled boom above me.

Anxiously I stared earthward. There it was! A huge white parachute drifted slowly toward the ground far below me, Vostok II easing her way toward the brown earth of a sprawling farm.

I dropped through the thin cloud layer, an air of joy and exultation sweeping through me. Now I could see small figures running across the ground, pointing to me as I swung in slow, graceful arcs beneath the parachute canopy. I looked down. Wonderful; no trees, houses, wires beneath me. I heard voices as I judged my landing site, then braced myself.

The earth rushed up and then my feet thudded into soft ground; I rolled over on my shoulder. I sat up quickly, laughing with the exhilaration of the moment. The parachute canopy collapsed about me like a flower gracefully folding enormous petals. I sat on the ground, simply overjoyed at the moment, laughing aloud. With my gloved hand I scooped up some earth and rubbed it gleefully against my face. It was wonderful!

The sounds of earth came to me . . . as though I had not heard them for years. The first thing I heard after the landing were the startled cries of birds, and then shouting in the distance. I glanced at my watch—eighteen minutes after ten o'clock. Exactly twenty-five hours and eighteen minutes ago I had left this same soil. It was hard to believe.

I climbed to my feet, brushing away the damp earth from the orange space suit. I laughed loudly at the first thing I saw . . . a man on a motorcycle bouncing madly across the plowed field, coming at me with full speed, shouting at the top of his lungs. From another side of the field a group of women ran toward me, their voices a chorus of excitement. And another sound; I turned my head to see an army jeep plowing its way across the field in a spray of earth.

The sense of excitement was overwhelming. I released the catches on the pressure gloves and dropped them to my feet. I could not resist the temptation; I held both arms aloft in a gesture of victory, grinning widely.

The jeep jerked to a stop, and two men almost fell out in their rush to reach me.

"Are you Titov?" they shouted in unison.

"The same!" I called out to them. They threw their arms about me, hugging me tightly and shouting in joy. Within seconds the group of women from the collective farm where I had landed were on the scene, and the babble of voices grew to pandemonium.

They helped me off with the space suit; we bundled the suit and the rolled-up parachute into the jeep and started out for the nearby road. The scene across that field was ludicrous, the jeep escorted by the motorcycle and the running women, horns blowing and everyone shouting at once. And through it all I inhaled deeply of the rich scent of the nearby forests and the fields. Say what you will about the "microclimate" atmosphere, nothing is quite so wonderful as Mother Earth.

The drive to a small army post was only two miles, but within seconds the road filled with cars, trucks, bicycles and motorcycles in a joyous impromptu convoy. The area was familiar to me, as well it should have been. Only several miles away, Yuri had landed here. We were in the Saratov region, near the official search and recovery headquarters of Krasney Koot, and as we drove along the highway to the army post, the drone of motors in the sky became louder and louder. Several helicopters drifted alongside the jeep on each side of the road, and I waved to the crews as I watched their grins and waves to me.

Vostok's automatic beacon transmitter was still beeping steadily, and the whine of jet engines pierced the sky as the high-altitude search planes came screaming low over the ground. One swept-wing fighter howled overhead and I craned my neck to look upward with a laugh as the pilot switched on his afterburner; with a blaze of flame and a deep hollow roar the airplane soared upward, rolling around and around in a salute to the safe return of our second spaceship.

Later, surrounded by a mob of officials and military personnel at the building where we had driven, I heard a sudden roar as a small group elbowed their way wildly through the crowd. The other cosmonauts had flown from Baikonur to the airstrip at Sverdlovsk, and then rushed at break-neck speed to join me. Now they burst through the swarming people and almost threw themselves at me. We pounded each other on the back, laughing and shouting in our excitement.

Then a general broke through the group; I had asked the moment I reached the building that a call be put through to Moscow, and the connection was now made. I ran inside the office and grasped the telephone; the operator said that the Soviet Premier was now coming to the phone.

His voice came to me clearly, with obvious pride. "Major Titov. . . . Congratulations!"

In the clipped, precise tones of an Air Force officer, as Yuri Gagarin had done before me at such a moment, I reported officially:

"Comrade General Secretary of the Central Committee of the Communist Party of the Soviet Union, I report that the task assigned to me by the Party and Government has been fulfilled. All equipment and installations in the spaceship worked perfectly. I have landed in the designated region, where I have been received very well. My condition is excellent."

There was a pause at the other end of the line, and then a wonderful, informal reply: "Remarkable, Major! You sound from your voice as though you have just been to a wedding ball."

The stiffness went out of me at his warmth. "Well, Nikita Sergeevitch," I said, "it was certainly a ball, but not a wedding ball."

There was loud laughter at the other end. For several minutes the Premier asked me questions of the flight, of my physical condition, and of my wife and family. He told me that a plane would be dispatched immediately to our home to bring my parents and sister to the capitol. His last words to me were, "We are waiting for you in Moscow. . . ."

The flight of Vostok II did not truly end with my safe return to earth. For several days the scientists and doctors of our program grilled me relentlessly to extract every possible detail of my mission in the cosmos. After the post-flight briefings I prepared exhaustive written reports—invaluable data to the engineers, scientists, mathematicians, doctors and biologists. To these men who would in turn expound upon my own information, and begin to establish the framework for another giant building block in our efforts to secure for man a permanent place in the vastness beyond this world of ours, the flight of Vostok II was but the second step of a great stairway leading to a dazzling future.

For me, of course, there came the deeply appreciated reception of the people of my country, from the highest levels of the government down to people from the smallest towns and villages.

I will never forget that long, long walk as I marched from my airplane over a narrow strip of red carpet laid on the surface of Vnukovo Airport. A walk along a carpet to signify the honors the Soviet Union wished to bestow upon me . . . upon the other cosmonauts . . . upon the vast team, many of them regretfully still unidentified, that has spurred the Soviet Union along the path to other worlds.

I walked that red carpet almost in a daze. About me were tens of thousands of faces, each of them giving forth with a roar that crashed almost physically against me, a thundering cry of welcome as I walked to the rostrum, to report personally and officially to Premier Khrushchev.

There will be with me forever the incredible din of the reception in Red Square . . . that wonderful reunion with Yuri . . . the moment we spent standing before hundreds of thousands of our people, with Premier Khrushchev's arms thrown about our shoulders.

Nothing can ever dim the memory of those breathtakingly beautiful sights in space. . . . Nothing can shake my conviction that a man knows this planet Earth only when he can see with his own eyes that sharp, rainbow circlet sweeping over the home of man.

Two other moments I will never forget.

The first is a period I spent with Cosmonaut 3, and the look of his eyes as he asked his piercing questions of my flight, as he prepared to stand this time before me, and to take the next step—outward.

That moment I will remember, just as I will remember one night several weeks after my return from space. Yuri and I were alone, walking the banks of a river beneath a sky glittering with stars.

We were, then, the only two men ever to have looked out upon space as we rushed around the planet below. But we did not talk of our flights; we had no need to do so.

Yuri started at the skies. "Gera, I spent the day yesterday with the Chief Constructor," he said quietly. "Our conversation was . . . quite remarkable."

He turned to look directly at me. "I want to tell you of the things we discussed."

"I want to tell you what he said about Mars. . . ."

Appendix I

Designation	Vostok II (Spacecraft VII)
Cosmonaut	Major Gherman Stephanovich Titov
Launch Date	August 6, 1961. 9:00 A.M. Moscow Time.
Recovery Date	August 7, 1961. 10:18 A.M. Moscow Time.
Booster Rocket	Two-stage. Engine clusters unknown. Dimensions unknown. Total thrust in excess of 1,300,000 lbs.
Payload (Vostok II) ...	10,408 lbs.
Payload Dimensions	Length approximately 22 feet. Diameter unknown.
Perigee	110.36 miles
Apogee	159.34 miles
Orbital Period	88.46 minutes
Total Orbits Vostok II ..	17.5
Total Mission Time	25 hours 18 minutes
Distance Traveled	436,937.31 miles
Booster Orbital Lifetime	(Stage II) Three days; re-entered atmosphere August 9th.
Orbit	Inclination 64 degrees 56 minutes to equator.

Communications .... Transmitters operated on:
15.765 megacycles
20.006 megacycles
19.995 megacycles (beacon only)
143.625 megacycles

Cabin Microclimate ..... Pressure: 1.05 atmospheres
Oxygen content: 24.33%
Temperature: 20-22° C.
Relative Humidity: 70-75%
Carbon Dioxide: 0.4%

Launch Site .... Baikonur

Recovery Site .... Krasney Koot, Saratov Region

° All flight figures are recalibrated estimates, and have been accepted officially for a world flight record by the Federation Aeronautique Internationale, of which the United States is an official member.

Appendix II

There are. throughout this story of Major Titov's flight in the Vostok II spaceship certain discrepancies with official sources and, perhaps more pertinent, with information concerned directly with Major Gagarin's flight of April 12, 1961 in the spaceship Vostok I. I believe it necessary to bring to the attention of the reader these various points so that the record might be kept fully-informed, so to speak.

Titov is emphatic on the point that he entered his spaceship thirty minutes before the scheduled firing time, and that Yuri Gagarin also entered Vostok I only thirty minutes prior to the scheduled launch. In his own recollections and descriptions of his flight, however, Gagarin lists the time as two hours prior to launch, when he sealed the hatch of his ship. My feeling is that the discrepancy here lies in inaccuracy of reporting and/or translation from Russian of passages relating to this particular incident. A thorough examination of all available sources pertaining to this pre-flight activity tends to support the time figure of Titov, but the matter of actual cosmonaut insertion into his spaceship prior to launch—in terms of time—still remains a question, and I do not feel it possible to resolve the question with the sources available.

A comparison is provided in the pre-flight activities of Lt. Colonel John H. Glenn, Jr., who orbited the earth three times in the Friendship 7 capsule on February 20, 1962. Colonel Glenn entered his spacecraft shortly after six A.M. The process of closing the Mercury capsule hatch is time-consuming, and Colonel Glenn endured a total of six delays and holds in his countdown. His launch occurred at 9:47 A.M. EST—not quite four hours after capsule insertion.

In his narrative Titov mentions only his presence at Baikonur when Gagarin made his flight; at no time does he refer to the other cosmonauts as being at the launch site. Gagarin, however, clearly states that all his fellow cosmonauts were present at his launching. I would ascribe this seeming discrepancy to the reports available from Titov, who does not state that the other cosmonauts were *not* with them. Here we seem to have an error of omission.

Another instance of omission is discernible in material from Gagarin; during their training period Gagarin describes his presence at Baikonur when he and the other cosmonauts personally witnessed the launching of one of the unmanned spacecraft with dogs inside the vehicle. Titov at no time brings up this subject.

The only men that Titov identifies by name during his preparations for flight are his two doctors; he makes no mention of the presence of his cosmonaut parachute instructor assisting him in donning all his equipment. Gagarin, however, specifically identifies Nikolai Konstantinovich as being present at his launch. Titov does not mention the instructor, who may or may not have been present during the launching of Vostok II.

In his narrative Titov shies from any specific number of training jumps he made while a cosmonaut; Gagarin is explicit on this by stating positively that he made "more than forty jumps in a short time."

Titov does not specify an exact landing area other than that he descended precisely where planned, near the recovery area for Gagarin. Gagarin, however, provides positive identification for his point of touchdown as "a field of the Leninsky Put Collective Farm, not far from the Smelovka village to the southwest of Engels."

The two preceding paragraphs again appear to be more omission than anything else.

And, once more, omission seems to apply to another incident. Titov states that when he flew from Baikonur with a general officer to meet Gagarin after he landed back on earth, that only he and the general went to the airplane for the flight. Or rather, he identifies only himself, the general, and the flight crew. He makes no mention of any of the other cosmonauts being with him when he greeted Gagarin—but Gagarin is explicit on the point that he was met by Titov "with the other men who had trained with me."

Again, the problems of interviews, reporters, translations, lack of understanding of the areas involved and misunderstandings seem to be the contributing factor in creating these seeming contradictions.

However, here I must provide a note of caution to the reader before a final departure. Many newsmen in this country, to say nothing of government officials and the average citizen, have seized upon such discrepancies as these—as well as others reported by different news media—as convincing proof that the flights of Gagarin and Titov truly are mockeries. These discrepancies are to them patent examples of the confusion suffered by the Russians in their fabrications of the two affairs.

To them, the Soviet system of information thus is exposed for its lies. By comparison, they point pridefully to our manner of reporting the flights of our astronauts. And they add with complete conviction that our reporting of the flights of Shepard, Grissom and Glenn suffers no such weaknesses as discrepancies or contradictions.

Having been a witness to launchings from Cape Canaveral for some twelve years, and having attended both as an observer and as a participant the great changes in the official attitude toward the press—many people forget that the press once was barred from the Cape, and they were barred for such purely scientific and "unsecret efforts" as Project Vanguard—I hold the greatest respect for and appreciation of the open manner in which the National Aeronautics and Space Administration "opened the gates" to the press for the flights of Shepard, Grissom and Glenn. Indeed, it is Congressional law that they carry out "maximum dissemination" of all activities relating to our civilian space program.

But for the pleasure and edification of the reader, I wish to bring to your attention certain "discrepancies" and "contradictions" that have attended these three man-in-space efforts. You are most likely in for a surprise . . .

First of all: Commander Alan B. Shepard, during his suborbital flight (MR-3) of May 5, 1961, *never* used the expression "A-OK" that was flashed around the world. Despite the use of this expression as a shining symbol of Shepard's flight, I repeat that at no time during his flight did Shepard ever say: "A-OK." Indeed, our first astronaut has specifically *denied* (at an open press conference) that he ever used this term.

If you will recall the flight of Astronaut Virgil I. Grissom, in his suborbital shot (MR-4) of July 21, 1961, you perhaps will remember that his space capsule hatch was secured to the spacecraft with explosive bolts. This is a specific description as provided by the National Aeronautics and Space Administration *in print*—on the very day of the launch.

In truth, however, Grissom's hatch was released from his capsule not by firing of explosive *bolts,* but through the firing of an explosive lanyard—a cord. It seems strange that the government should issue an official statement that the capsule contained explosive bolts when it did not have this equipment.

For some time after Grissom's recovery from the ocean great confusion existed specifically on his danger while swimming in the sea. Refer back to that day and you will read account after account that cheeringly consoles us with the news that he was never in any danger. In truth—his space suit was filling rapidly with sea water through an open suit port, he was sinking lower and lower into the sea, and the doctor who helped him to disrobe from his suit stated specifically that Grissom "came within thirty to sixty seconds of drowning."

There are many others—virtually all of them honest errors, a few of them the result of some inevitable bureaucratic meddling with information. If you believed that John Glenn in his capsule atop the Atlas rocket prior to launch had the ability to escape from an emergency by firing his capsule rocket himself—then you are wrong. Virtually every reporter at Cape Canaveral believed that all Glenn had to do was to pull the escape rocket firing control, and his rocket would lift him off the Atlas.

This is absolutely false—until forty-five seconds before liftoff. Until that time Glenn lacked this escape capability; he pulled the firing control, a light flashed in the blockhouse and in Mercury control, a man at a panel had to activate an escape-system lead, and *then* Glenn's escape rocket would fire. A minor point? Not if that Atlas had exploded.

At a press conference at the NASA Press Center in the Starlite Motel at Cocoa Beach, Florida, I questioned a top engineer from the McDonnell Aircraft Company about the escape system of the capsule during the countdown. I was told—in the presence of four hundred newsmen, and it was taped—that before Glenn could fire his escape rocket, the power cables leading to the capsule from the service tower first had to be ejected from the capsule. Otherwise, the engineer stated emphatically, the results to the capsule and to Glenn would be "quite catastrophic."

As it turned out, other engineers disclaimed (rather violently, I might add) this statement, and said that it was ridiculous—that the capsule *could* be fired with the power cables still attached; that a pressure-sensing device would spring them free during the escape rocket firing.

It turns out that the latter engineers were correct, that the man addressing the four hundred newsmen did *not* have his story correct. But that *was* the story that went out through the United States and to the rest of the world.

Enjoying the protection of a free press as we do, and which we must have, does not provide a guarantee that the information reported will always be correct, or that it will not contain discrepancies or contradictions. For, in truth, sometimes it does.

And one final point. Not even the presence of the free press is a panacea for the distribution of official *mis*information.

MARTIN CAIDIN